S0-BQX-9

Music in Practice

edited by Paul Kramer

Oxford University Press
Music Department, Walton Street, Oxford OX2 6DP

Also by Paul Farmer
Music in the Comprehensive School
A Handbook of Composers and their Music

Collection and editorial © Paul Farmer 1984

First published 1984

Reprinted 1986

ISBN 0 19 321094 0

Acknowledgements

We are grateful to the following for permission to reproduce their material:

Chappell Music Ltd. ('Heart and Soul' from *A Song is Born*, music by Hoagy Carmichael, words by Frank Loesser © 1938 Famous Music Corp. British publisher Famous Chappell; 'I got Rhythm' from *Girl Crazy*, music by George Gershwin, words by Ira Gershwin © 1930 New World Corp. British publisher Chappell Music Ltd.); G. Ricordi & Co. Ltd. (It's Now or Never', arrangement of 'O sole mio' by E. D. di Capua with English words by Aaron Schroeder and Wally Gold).

The photographs on pages 40 and 96 are by permission of the B.B.C. and *Child Education*. All others are by Keith Hawkins.

Printed in Hong Kong

Contents

Introduction

This is a practical book for music teachers. It is not a collection of grand-sounding philosophies of music education, nor does it have a 'creative' or 'traditional' bias. It is simply a collection of good ideas for the secondary music classroom, described by teachers who are 'experts' in their particular fields.

In compiling these chapters I have tried to cover not only the regular aspects of school music (such as instrumental work, singing and listening to music) but also some unusual ones. For example, most teachers will understandably not have either bothered or wanted to involve their classes in medieval or Indian music; yet the ideas in this book on these topics and all the other aspects of music teaching will soon show the reader that such work *is* possible in any school.

However, while this book can certainly be treated as a source of ideas to be 'dipped into' at any time, it should *not* simply be considered as a collection of ready-made lessons to be used in exactly the same way wherever and whenever the lessons take place. All the contributors have stressed that their ideas have evolved *from their own situation*, and that they may well not 'work' elsewhere, at least not all the time.

We should all strive to organize our music teaching in the best possible way, and while that includes a continual search for new and better ideas and methods (which is where I hope this book will help), it does not mean simply copying other people's lessons and fitting them into one's own teaching in a haphazard or illogical way.

For these reasons I hope that this book will not encourage teachers to ignore their own responsibility to plan their music teaching, but that it will be a useful source of new material that they can develop and improve in the most appropriate way for their own classes.

PAUL FARMER

Notes on contributors

Paul Farmer was Head of Music at two London comprehensive schools in the 1970s, including Holland Park School where he developed the first CSE exam in pop music. He later took an MA in Curriculum Studies at the London University Institute of Education, where he is currently researching into the influence of the 'new technology' on the curriculum. He has written widely on secondary school music, including textbooks, articles and a personal view, *Music in the Comprehensive School* (OUP). He is currently Deputy Head of Dick Sheppard School, London.

Trevor Davies was Head of Music for four years at Rutherford School, London NW1. There he developed courses which were designed to encourage the widest possible musical involvement of all pupils in a multi-racial, inner-city school. He recently spent a year of related study and research in the music department of the London University Institute of Education.

Margaret O'Shea is a divisional music co-ordinator in the ILEA. It was through her work at the ILEA Centre for Young Musicians and at Walsingham School, Clapham (where she was Head of Music), that she became particularly interested in the Kodály method and its application to English-speaking children. She recently represented the ILEA at the Kodály international conference in Sydney.

Grenville Hancox taught at Madeley Court School, Shropshire, from its opening in 1971. During 1979–80 he was the dissemination officer for the Schools Council project *Music in the Secondary School Curriculum*, the work of his department featuring largely in the output of the project. He now lectures at Christ Church College, Canterbury.

Michael Burnett is Principal Lecturer and Head of Music at Southlands College, Roehampton Institute of Higher Education, and was on secondment to the Jamaica School of Music as Senior Tutor from 1978–81. He is editor of *Music Education Review*, writer and presenter of the BBC Schools' programme, *Music Box*, and has a wide range of published works to his credit.

Tony Attwood was until recently a Senior Lecturer in Music at Dartington College of Arts. He was previously a Head of Music in London, before working at the Cockpit Theatre, from where he encouraged the development of pop music in many London schools. He has been responsible for several school textbooks on pop, and is now a publisher with Hamilton House Publishing.

Phil Ellis taught music in comprehensive schools for ten years. The last seven of these were spent as Head of Music at Notley High School in Essex, where he also became involved with the Schools Council project *Music in the Secondary School Curriculum*. He is at present lecturing at Huddersfield Polytechnic, where he is in charge of the electronic music studio.

Joan Arnold's first job was as Head of Music at Horndean School, Hampshire, where she became particularly interested in the integration of Music, Art and Drama. In 1977 she moved to her present post as Head of Faculty of Creative Arts' Studies at Frogmore School, Surrey, where she is responsible for the oversight of the art, drama and music departments.

Brian Dennis first gained a reputation as a music educator with the publication of *Experimental Music in Schools*, and has since lectured in various parts of the world as well as throughout Britain. He currently lectures in composition and music education at Royal Holloway College, London University, and has over 100 songs and two chamber operas to his credit.

Roy Bennett spent twenty years teaching Music, Drama, French and English Literature in a variety of schools. The last seven of these years were as Head of Music and Drama at a comprehensive school in Somerset, where he developed his highly successful series of textbooks, *Enjoying Music* (Longman). He has now retired from teaching to take up full-time writing.

Leela Floyd was born in Singapore and went to secondary school in England. After studying at The Royal Academy of Music she made a special study of music in India. She has since taught in a variety of schools, and recently completed a Leverhulme scholarship research project, at the London University Institute of Education, on music education in multi-racial schools.

Peter West has worked at the GLC's Cockpit theatre and arts workshop since 1976, when he finished studying at the Royal College of Music. He began working exclusively with electronic music, which he helped to develop in several ILEA schools; more recently he has broadened his work with young people to include Rock and Reggae at the Lisson Green music workshop.

Music in an inner-city school

Trevor Davies

In this first chapter, Trevor Davies offers four different ideas for classroom music which have 'worked' at Rutherford School in the centre of London. Rutherford was a boys' secondary school (designated 'social priority') until its reorganization in 1980 as part of the new North Westminster School.

The title of this chapter begs the question, 'What is there in particular about an inner-city school?', and while Trevor Davies has a good deal of experience of inner-city pupils, he admits that it is difficult to describe 'their uniqueness':

> *'They live in a noisy, fast-moving, harsh environment with limited horizons. The hall-mark of their behaviour is a strident impatience and an untiring enthusiasm.'*

At first sight an inner-city school may seem to be rich territory for a multi-ethnic approach to music teaching, and while there are opportunities in some schools for work along these lines, for example tackling Indian music (see p. 96), most pupils wherever they live seem more anxious to embrace the mass culture of Western Europe. This was certainly what Trevor Davies found at Rutherford. His approach was therefore geared towards music in what he describes as the 'popular-standard' tradition, making use of the 'bread and butter' ingredients which have been the mainstay of popular music throughout this century.

These projects are reports on work developed in the classroom, rather than lesson material prepared in advance, and Trevor Davies' pupils have therefore played an important role in determining the projects' outcome in his own school. Because of this he has suggested that they should be treated as 'ideas for growth rather than hermetically sealed instant lessons'. What is special about them is that they have proved successful in the inner-city school, a particularly demanding teaching situation. They should therefore be a very useful starting point for classwork in any school.

PROJECT 1

Peripatetic team-teaching

One of the chief difficulties with lively pupils is to get the music started. Pupils who are by nature unsettled will seldom have the patience to refrain from playing their instruments while I teach another group. To combat this I decided to involve my peripatetic teachers in a team-led lesson. The second year class in question was, on the one hand, more musical than any other in its year, and on the other, the most boisterous.

The specialisms offered by the teachers were: guitar, bass guitar, saxophone and clarinet, keyboard with tuned percussion, and percussion; in addition to myself, there was another teacher who volunteered to assist setting up. Obviously the class was extraordinarily staffed, and in effect was getting about six lessons in one. As it transpired, they achieved in one lesson immeasurably more than in six normal lessons.

The team met at the beginning of the lunch hour which preceded the lesson, in order to devise the piece. These considerations were borne in mind:

Instrumentation

a 'Specialist' pupils available: 1 clarinet; 2 tenor saxophones; 1 rhythm guitar; an absolute beginner on electric bass who was to have his first try on the instrument; 1 percussion pupil who was to play snare with brushes.
b Classroom instruments: 4 tuned percussion; 1 chord organ.

Who plays what?

Not to have this sorted out in advance is to court disaster! Because we were using instructors who already taught pupils in this class, it only remained to decide upon the tuned percussion and organ.

The style of the piece

We settled on a blues style, as there are three chords with plenty of scope for repetition. The blues is an idiom into which can be fitted simple parts, and one for which the pupils have great affinity because of its use in many kinds of rock and pop music. In this particular case we extended the usual 12-bar blues to 16 bars.

Key

There is a conflict of interest if one is to provide simple parts for guitar as well as B flat instruments. We decided on C, substituting Cm or Dm for the F7 chord. F7 is a difficult chord, but Cm implies F7/9, and Dm implies F6. In fact, professional players often make these substitutions anyway.

The workshop groups

Pupils were divided as follows:
a   Xylophones, glockenspiels and chord organ.
b   Snare drum (2 players).
c   Rhythm guitar, bass guitar.
d   2 saxophones, 1 clarinet.

The piece was then written and scored, with each teacher advising on the capabilities of his or her instrument. Separate parts were written out, although we knew that these would be used more by the tutors than the pupils, who would probably learn their parts by rote.

At the beginning of the lesson, we played the piece to the class, who were delighted by its title, *2G Blues*. We explained the function of the various parts (lead, harmony, bass and rhythm) and played them separately before performing the piece together again. The class then divided for the workshop session.

Each teacher had a group. Groups A and B worked in the same room. As the tuned percussion learned their parts, the snare drum line was developed from a

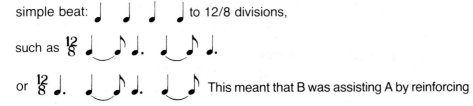

This meant that B was assisting A by reinforcing the pulse, and A was helping B by providing the part against which the beat was to be played. (A rhythm part can so often seem irrelevant on its own.)

Groups C and D worked separately. The guitar teacher had problems teaching rhythm guitar as well as bass to an absolute beginner, and the woodwind teacher had to concentrate on the saxophone line to the exclusion of the clarinet. As I did not have a group, I was able to help wherever necessary, for example in writing a new part for the clarinet.

The workshop lasted about half an hour, which left time for the class to re-assemble. Having mastered their parts they were able to perform as a full ensemble, and were clearly highly motivated and gratified by their achievement. The arrangement as we used it would obviously require modification for use with any other group, though in fact I would envisage a different product anyway each time this approach is used. The opportunity to sweep aside the inherent frustrations of attempting a piece like this with a class and to give them an intensive musical experience was clearly worth while. It was also interesting to bring the instrumental teachers into the classroom, and open the pupils' eyes to the potential satisfaction of learning an instrument. Such a project is not without its own special problems, though, not least of which is arranging a suitable day for peripatetic teachers to come to the school together. However, it should be noted that the teachers found the project worth repeating several times in the year.

Trevor Davies

PROJECT 2

Further use of the blues

Making use of the normal classroom instruments with any orchestral instruments available, everyone can start with the same line:

Ex. 2

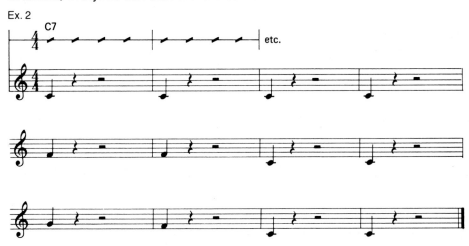

The class can be taught by rote, or from a diagram on the board. You can see that by taking it as three groups of four bars, the third and fourth bar of each line is the same. This helps to establish the structure in the pupil's mind.

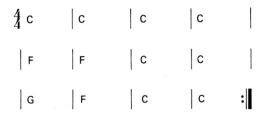

Here is a suggested accompaniment for the teacher:

Ex. 3

11

One quarter note on the first beat of each bar is greatly improved by substituting two eighth notes:

Ex. 4

This sounds very effective on xylophone and piano, whilst the more sustained instruments (recorders or glockenspiels) can try:

Ex. 5

Here is a good line for clarinet or saxophone, which will need transposing accordingly:

Ex. 6

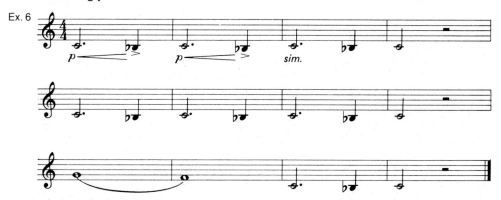

The bass line, on piano, tuned percussion or bass guitar, can 'walk' up to the new chords:

Ex. 7

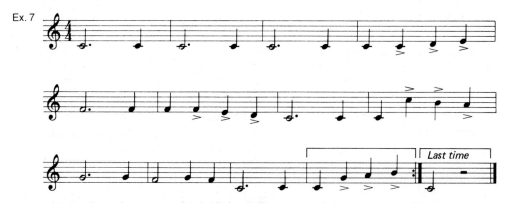

The bass can also be played on timps, or tunable 'Timp-Toms'. Riffs can be introduced to highlight chord changes:

Ex. 8

A melodic 'question and answer' can be set up as an extension to Ex. 4.

Ex. 9

Choose a few of these ideas at a time, bringing them in gradually, and thus extending the range of the piece in performance. An important factor easily neglected is *tempo*. All too often we sing and play in class at a 'working tempo' which can make the music rather dull. Playing the blues is an excellent opportunity to teach the pupils to play at a very slow tempo, or a well-controlled fast one.

PROJECT 3

A drama presentation with music

This project, which involved two second year classes, resulted in a 12–14 minute performance. One class devised the play, and the other performed the music. The play was a burlesque about a bank robbery in a Western town. The pupils worked out the story and the scenes themselves and it was, quite simply, very funny. I include an outline of the plot, although the synopsis does not do it justice!

The gang are having tea in their hideout, and encouraged by 'Ma' to 'get along and do something instead of sitting around here all day', they hit upon the idea of robbing the bank. One of them, 'Tubs', whose mind is always on food, has the job of going to the Telegraph Office to warn the Sheriff that there is a robbery in the *next* town, to divert his attention. 'Tubs' is a little slow on the uptake, and, predictably, gets it wrong. He arrives at the Telegraph Office and sends a wire, 'Bank being robbed'. The Sheriff gets the cable and reluctantly leaves his warm office to investigate. While he is on his way the gang rob the bank and when he gets there with his deputies it is all over. The gang get to their hideout and count their loot: 248 dollars and 59 cents. 'O.K.', calls the leader of the gang, 'Play the music'. The band, however, will not play. One of their number goes up onto the stage: 'We've been playing in this lousy show for six months, and we ain't been paid!'
'O.K., how much do we owe you?'
'248 dollars and 59 cents.'
He takes the money and the band play the theme music.

The pupils exploited many possibilities of character portrayal in each scene and it was this that made the performance. Each scene was described in frames projected on an overhead projector, in the style of the silent films. This made the performance easier to understand and set the mood.

The theme music was written by me for another class, and was an extension of an improvised sequence. Making use of a pupil who plays guitar to give a solid backing to the sound of class instruments, we evolved this passage:

Ex. 10

Trevor Davies

With the robust sound of the electric guitar, someone said that it sounded like music for a Western, and this chance remark brought the two classes together for a performance. I wrote a very simple theme tune based upon the above example:

Ex. 11

Moderato

Melody (Trumpet)

Bass (Tuned percussion)

Snare drum

The tuned percussion part was written like this:

| — | E | A | E | A | D | G | D | G etc. |

A little time out of class was required for practice, but the bulk of the work was done in lessons. In addition to the theme tune, there were very short incidental parts. The advantage of using music with a play is that the simplest of musical ideas can be employed, though even a single sound has to be perfectly timed. It is hard to make this point understood in terms of absolute music, but the drama element provides the framework, the discipline, and the motivation. Here are two brief incidental sections that were used, both separately and as a sequence:

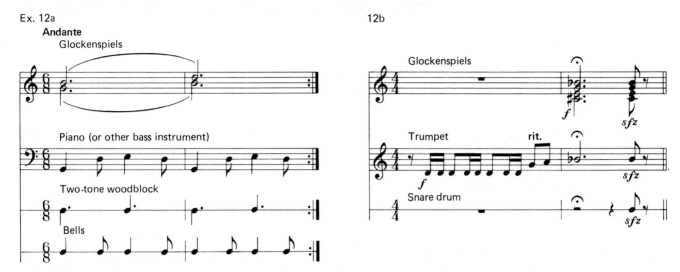

Ex. 12a   12b

Ex. 12(a) was used twice. The delivery of the telegram and the sheriff's journey from his office to the bank involved 'riding' right round the hall in a deliberate 'jogalong' manner. (This was very funny to watch because the sets were fixed on stage, all next to each other, whilst the route taken by the actors was the longest possible!) Ex. 12(b) was for moments of excitement; namely, the entry of the robbers, and later the sheriff, to the bank. The stylized nature of the music was obviously reflected in the portrayal of the action and the characters.

The final performance, presented in a school assembly, provided a common goal which greatly aided the pupils' concentration and commitment. Without that objective they possibly would not have overcome the final hurdle that transformed *The Robbery* from a classroom workshop idea into a successful presentation, involving half the members of one year group.

PROJECT 4

Singing

In my own experience secondary pupils are reluctant to sing these days. Whether something unusual happens to the vocal chords of the inner-city child I do not know, but I do know that they find it difficult to sing well in tune, and that interesting ventures, such as part singing, they find very hard indeed. I have however had success with 'scat' singing over simple chord sequences, building up the harmony and even adding a tune.

Many teachers will have used vocal music as a basis for instrumental work, but it can also be tried the other way round. Take this simple phrase on tuned percussion:

Ex. 13

Then sing it to the 'words':

> Doo-Dah Doo-Wah; Doo-Dah Doo-Wah

Now sing this one:

Ex. 14

Trevor Davies

These two ideas can be combined, by singing or playing, while the teacher can accompany on guitar or piano. You will find a tendency for the pupils to make the fourth note too short, which can spoil the flow of the music. Leave that for a moment and teach the class *Heart and Soul*, not with any words, but like this:

Ex. 15a

Now divide the class into three: lead, firsts and seconds. The seconds start with Ex. 13 and the firsts come in four bars later with Ex. 14; after another four bars, in comes the tune. Naturally, each group has a go at each part.

Ex. 15b

Scat singing over a chord sequence need not be intended to fit a complete tune, but can also be learned and embellished for its own sake. Here is another example:

Ex. 16

with a counter melody

Ex. 17

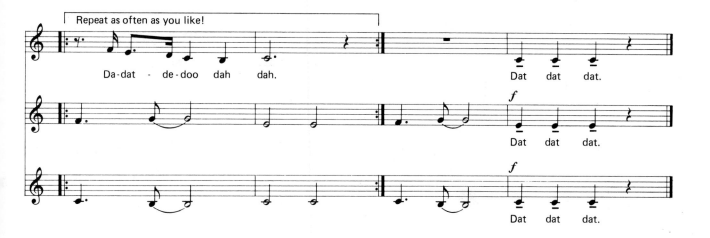

which goes in canon:

Ex. 18

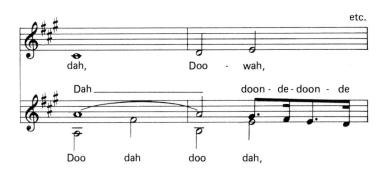

The original line (Ex. 16) can be put to a more interesting scat figure:

Ex. 19

This is plenty here to work on for its own interest, but it can also be used against the melody *Blue Moon*, with one of the above as an eight-bar introduction before bringing in the tune over Ex. 19.

Allowing for a few adjustments, you could also use this line to 'I've got rhythm': even the middle eight should not cause too much difficulty. The arrangement below may look very hard, but I have found that it lies within the scope of a moderately good class.

Ex. 20

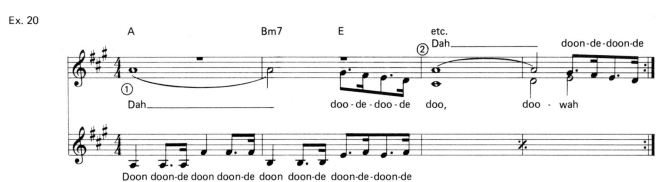

Use a simple chordal accompaniment and encourage the pupils to sing in a relaxed manner. Forget the traditional goals of intensity of tone and projection for the moment; the aim here is to get them singing in tune. This is a style which developed with the microphone, and if you have mikes, use them. For the pupils, singing without a mike is unusual! Using this style it is possible to coax them into a more accurate response to pitch and a more fluent use of their singing voices. The repeated, catchy phrases and the absence of words, together with the relaxed atmosphere of the music, draws them into this activity. If possible, use brushes on a snare drum, or sandpaper blocks to embellish the backing.

Other tunes that make use of repeated chord sequences are:

Tiptoe through the Tulips   EMI
The Way you look tonight   Chappell
Words of Love (Buddy Holly)   Music Sales
Everyday (Buddy Holly)   Music Sales
You won't see me (Lennon/McCartney)   Northern Songs
This Boy (Lennon/McCartney)   Northern Songs
Love is the Sweetest Thing   EMI

Related bibliography

D. Machel: 'All Together Now, 1 2 3' *Music Teacher*, Jan. 1980
An excellent description of a well-thought-out approach to practical music with secondary pupils, along the lines of my own work. Pupils are encouraged to devise their own harmony as well as read 'semi-conventional' parts.

S. Pavey: 'Instrumental Teaching in the Classroom' *Music Teacher*, July 1980
A suggested approach for the instrumental specialist which encourages your peripatetics into the classroom!

K. Swanwick: *Popular Music and the Teacher* Pergamon Press, 1968
The first appraisal of the possibilities open to the teacher who ventures across cultural barriers.

P. Farmer: *Ragtime & Blues* Longman, 1979
A very short textbook which includes classroom Blues pieces, suitable for 1st–3rd year pupils.

Singing

Margaret O'Shea

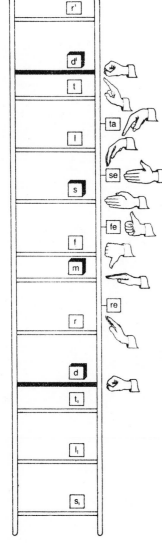

It is widely believed that singing in secondary schools is dead, at least in ordinary class music lessons. In the traditional sense this may be true to some extent: in the 1980s teenagers may understandably be reluctant to sing apparently irrelevant and out-of-date songs from old-fashioned-looking songbooks. However, those teachers prepared to experiment with fresh ideas for class singing have had a good deal of success (see Music in an inner-city school *and* The uses of pop*). Here Margaret O'Shea suggests two highly original approaches to the problem.*

The first section of this chapter describes a series of activities, many of which are practised world-wide by teachers who make use of the Kodály method. It is intended that only a few of these activities be used at a time in lessons which may include other forms of singing or instrumental work.

Part of the aim of this work is to attain precise tuning and recognition of different pitches, so initially the musical materials used are very simple. Pupils need regular practice over a period of time before they absorb each step thoroughly, and 'a little and often' is certainly a successful maxim.

It is this element of practice within a progressive programme of work which is so basic to the traditions of instrumental teaching but often lacking in our classrooms. Yet research in America, Hungary and Australia has shown that through working regularly for short periods, young children will equal the performance of pupils five and six years their senior who have not had Kodály training in rhythmic memory, improvisation and sight-singing. Margaret O'Shea's own experience in secondary schools has shown that this work can make a tremendous difference to pupils' aural perception. She claims that five to ten minutes, even once a week, for the first three years of the secondary school, will 'sharpen the capacity to listen and the ability to concentrate'.

The singing-drama work described in the second part of this chapter takes a whole lesson. Indeed, it will only be successful when a series of lessons working in this way enables a group to build up confidence and experience. It might therefore be best tackled as a half-term project. Apart from the fact that pupils can gain a sense of the natural musical flow of language through this work, it also opens the door to an enjoyment and appreciation of the world of opera.

PART 1

Using Kodály Methods

Pitch training

First, introduce the *solfa* names and sounds of *doh, me* and *soh* with the corresponding hand signals.

doh   ray   me   fah   soh   lah   te   doh

I have found it useful to encourage pupils to use both hands when making the hand signals. After some 'dodging' on these, when the class is singing confidently, give a small group a sung ostinato pattern to sustain, for example:

Then, with hand signals, guide the class in singing a melody accompanied by this ostinato:

Through hand signals, teach this simple two-part round.

A very enjoyable game, which helps to develop internal memory of pitch, is the **piano game**. Divide the class into a three-note 'piano' and play the 'Jubilate' round on it by pointing to each group who must immediately sing their note. You will probably have plenty of volunteers who will want to 'play' the choral 'piano' or try singing a note on their own.

Another game which will have the class on their toes, is singing the round in unison to solfa, but with every *me* silent. Then repeat it with every *doh* silent. Try also singing the melody in unison until a signal is given. Continue singing silently in the mind until a further signal is given and the melody may become audible again. Everyone should have reached the same place! This can be great fun to try when singing in two parts or more.

Constantly bring the class to an awareness of the tuning and quality of the notes they are singing. Building a four-note chord is one way of focusing their precise attention. Ask the whole class to sing *doh*, then, while a quarter of the group hold this note, the rest of the class sing the top *doh*. Leave another quarter of the class on this note and bring the remaining half down to *soh*, then, finally, add *me* with the last group.

It is a good idea to sing these notes with an open, generous 'Ah' which makes it easy to take a breath when needed. This is a most satisfying excercise which demands breath control and careful listening to one's own voice.

Gradually introduce higher and lower notes of the chord through hand signals. Make it clear, by the height of the hands in the air, which *doh*, *me* or *soh* you mean.

Teach this three-part round through hand signals.

Round (entries marked *)

Al - le - lu - ia,   Al - le - lu - ia,   Al - le - lu - ia,   Al - le - lu - ia.

Training in rhythm

While receiving this initial practice in pitch training, pupils also need to master some basic rhythmic patterns. These may be taught through use of word rhythms or through use of time names:

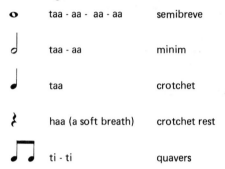

𝅝	taa - aa - aa - aa	semibreve
𝅗𝅥	taa - aa	minim
𝅘𝅥	taa	crotchet
𝄽	haa (a soft breath)	crotchet rest
𝅘𝅥𝅮𝅘𝅥𝅮	ti - ti	quavers

Whichever method is preferred, it is useful to make a series of cards with combinations of patterns written sufficiently clearly for the whole class to see:

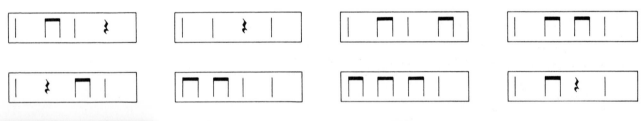

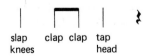

A rest sign

I have found it useful to first teach rhythms as written above and to start writing the complete notes at a later stage. These shapes are so easy to draw, that pupils can write them almost at the speed they hear them.

When clapping these patterns, pupils should use a definite sideways movement of the hands to indicate a rest.

When pupils are used to being dodged in clapping these rhythms, sing a round and use a pattern as an ostinato, first of all performed by a group as the others sing, then by the whole class clapping and singing simultaneously. Pupils enjoy being able to do two things at once and will like the challenge of quickly extending this to three! Try tapping the beat with the toe and clapping an ostinato while singing the round! Also, the class may be divided and perform several ostinati simultaneously:

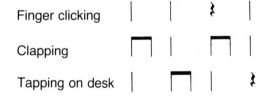

Finger clicking

Clapping

Tapping on desk

Some of the techniques already learnt can begin to be combined. For example,

| | | |
slap   clap clap   tap
knees   head

establish an ostinato, such as knees, clap, tap head, and then commence singing the round, making silent every note that coincides with the beat on the knees. Then perform again, singing *only* that beat!

Further reinforcement of the sense of beat can be given by asking the pupils to stand in pairs. One pupil can walk the beat on the spot while the other taps the rhythm of the song being sung on his or her partner's shoulders.

Sight-reading

The class should now be ready to try some sight-reading. First, give them a rhythm to read with time names and clapping:

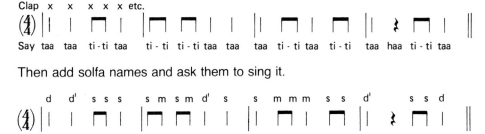

Then add solfa names and ask them to sing it.

It is also useful to make a series of small cards, on each of which is a single symbol.

If each pupil is given a small pack they can quickly arrange them in patterns given orally by the teacher or a member of the class.

Extending the range of pitch

The range of notes used can gradually be extended as pupils add to their repertoire of songs. For example, *re* is added when learning:

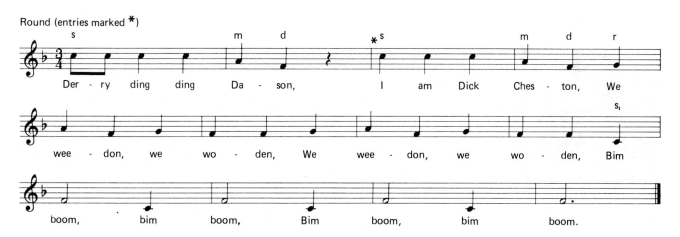

The note *te* can be added with:

One of the problems at this stage is that one may find the song that is exactly right for a certain class's musical development, but be faced with the sure knowledge that 2C will never sing words such as 'ding, dong, ding, dong, dong'! In such a case, I frequently make up short rhymes, possibly completely idiotic in content, but relevant to the class in question.

Musically, by now, pupils should be able to sight-read this material if given rhythm and solfa names.

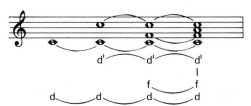

Each new song should be practised in solfa and with hand signals.

To do the hand signals while singing the words and while singing the song as a round helps to develop the automatic use of them. Rhythmically, pupils should be beginning to work out their own ostinati patterns to accompany their songs, either with body rhythms, or performed on unpitched instruments.

Another chord can now be practised as before:

To reinforce the sense of where the note comes in the octave try singing songs to the numbers of the notes in the octave as well as to the solfa names.

Alleluia

Mozart

To sing a song such as this to numbers brings home to the pupil the idea of going 'up and down' which is not necessarily clear, even at secondary age. It is interesting to note the number of pupils who will happily sing:

Using the stave

As soon as pupils can easily sing any note to a given hand signal, and are showing a clear sense of direction when ascending and descending scale-like passages, they are ready to become accustomed to the stave, first by reading patterns over one line.

Other lines of the stave may be added gradually, according to the speed of the class. Songs may also be practised with pupils pointing to their fingers and the spaces between for the lines and spaces of the stave.

Practice at writing down easy patterns or songs which have been learnt also helps to consolidate what the pupils are learning aurally.

This is a good point for revision of songs already learnt but now written out on a complete stave. It is particularly useful to practise the two chords,

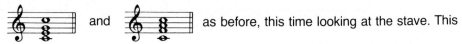

and   as before, this time looking at the stave. This

helps to train the eye to recognize leaps as well as consecutive notes.

As soon as the class is used to reading all the lines and spaces in solfa or numbers they will find it simple to learn the letter names of the notes.

This means songs may now be performed in a number of ways.

'Frère Jacques'

d	r	m	d
line	space	line	line
	(between thumb and forefinger)		

Words	Since	sing -	ing	is	so	good	a	thing	I	wish	all	men	would	learn	to	sing.
Solfa	s	d'	d'	d'	s	t	l	s	m	s	f	m	r	d	d	d
Numbers	5	8	8	8	5	7	6	5	3	5	4	3	2	1	1	1
Names	G	C	C	C	G	B	A	G	E	G	F	E	D	C	C	C
Time	Taa	taa - aa	taa	taa - aa	taa	etc.										

Pupils can clap a beat, clap a rhythm and 'think' a silent bar.

Make cards saying:

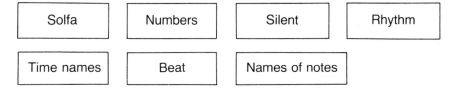

As pupils sing the song, hold up cards so that they have to change the way of performing the song without stopping the performance. The result may be something like this:

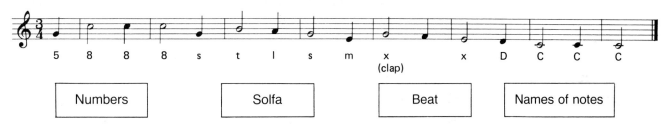

This can be riotously funny in class but, when slickly performed, can make an impressive demonstration on open day!

While singing the tune, pupils will now enjoy a similar activity with ostinati cards. Have several in your hands and keep changing them, so that pupils have to constantly clap a different rhythm while keeping the song going. An extension of this, which is excellent memory training, is to give some members of the class a card to hold and stand them facing the others. While they all sing a song, point to each of these chosen pupils so that the class changes the pattern they are clapping. Then turn these pupils round with their backs to the class and see if the class can remember the patterns as you continue to point to the individual pupils with cards and the class continues to sing.

A game which is a useful test of pitch memory is the **dice game**. The class is divided into two teams sitting in a row, each with a leader who is equipped with a pitched instrument. The leader sounds a *doh* and then throws a dice. The member of the team must sing the note indicated by the dice (e.g. *me* if the dice lands on three). The corresponding member of the opposition team may judge if the note sung was correct. Final judgment is made by the leader of the team who sounds the note on his instrument. A mark is given to the team if the note is sung correctly. A mark may also be given to whoever makes the correct judgment.

Compound time

So far we have been using patterns in simple time only. As the rhythms of compound time are so natural to the English language it is important to introduce some songs in compound time as soon as possible.

Time names used will be as follows:

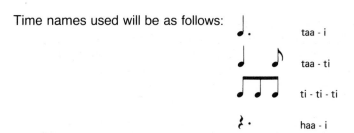

It is important that no idea be created in pupils' minds that these rhythms are difficult or more advanced. Change freely from repertoire in simple time to that in compound time and use all the techniques that pupils have so far mastered: using sung or clapped ostinati; changing from performing the beat to performing the rhythm; using silent bars and sight-reading short passages. Pupils may now be ready for two ostinati at once while singing a song:

Ask them to change parts on a given signal. This is difficult to do; make sure you've practised it yourself, first!

Minor tonality

With hand signals, lead the class in exploring the downward fall from *doh* to *la* and the sound of the minor chord.

Repertoire in the *la* mode (aeolian) is excellent preparation for mastering minor tonality.

Round (entries marked *)   Praetorius

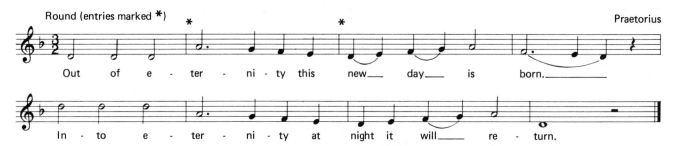

Out of e - ter - ni - ty this new__ day__ is born.____

In - to e - ter - ni - ty at night it will____ re - turn.

Singing in harmony

To be able to lead the class in two-part singing through hand signals may need some practice first (perhaps in front of a mirror!), but it is the easiest way I know of introducing a class to harmony.

Half the class follows the signals given by your left hand and half the class follows your right hand. At first, try this moving over a chord:

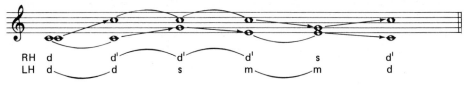

RH d   d'   d'   d'   s   d'
LH d   d   s   m   m   d

Then introduce some consecutive movement.

RH d   r   m   f   s   s   s   f   m
LH d   d   d   d   d   r   m   r   d

There are tremendous advantages in working in this way. You have complete freedom to wait on each harmony until the group has it in tune. Any pupils holding a long note must give their full attention to its tuning and quality of sound, otherwise its pitch will alter. If you indicate a note for a group to sing and the pupils find it too difficult, you can immediately signal for them to join the other half of the class in a unison, and then proceed again or signal a note which you know they will be able to find easily. Changes of pitch can be as slow as are necessary. Pupils have time to listen to the harmony they are making, and enjoy it!

An extension of this exercise is to divide the class into two or three groups, each with a leader. With an unpitched instrument give the class a very regular beat. The leader of each group will give a hand signal on every fourth beat and that group will sing the appropriate note. Initially they can try this using the notes of the chord but, as they become more experienced, this can develop into a most demanding musical exercise when they use all the notes of the octave.

Finally, here is a game which it is possible to adapt to your own resources.

Solfa assault course

Cut out very large cardboard shapes in different colours, each shape to represent one solfa sound. For example:

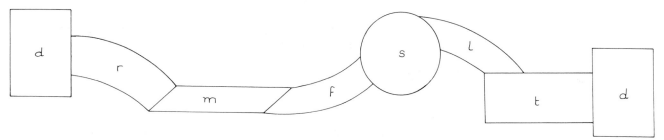

Make sure the whole pattern will fit across the floor of your music room. Then, by walking and jumping around on the cards, dodge the class in their singing of solfa.

To play the game, you need 12 pieces of card labelled, threateningly:
(a) someone is throwing fast staccato at you (b) a crescendo engulfs you (c) you nearly disappear in a diminuendo (d) a tremolo troubles you (e) solfa maniacs won't stop singing soh-me (f) you are plucked by a pizzicato (g) an ostinato gets louder and louder (h) *con fuoco* nearly scorches your clothes (i) a *glissando* glides down your spine (j) you are frightened by a *ffz* (k) you reach despair – this note won't stop (l) an *appassionato* distracts you.

These are only examples – I am sure you can think of suitably frightening messages!

Practise the sounds indicated by the cards, either with free vocal sounds or with instruments, or both. Then distribute the cards on either side of the solfa cards *re* to *te*. The class should be divided into small groups, each responsible for one card.

Place a blindfolded pupil on the bottom *doh*. He or she must attempt to walk slowly up the assault course and reach top *doh*. The pupil is guided by the whole class who sing the note being stood on. As soon as the pupil places a foot even a fraction over the edge, the others on that side threaten him or her with the sound indicated by their instruction card, so that he or she knows to change direction!

PART 2

Singing – drama

Starting points

Sung drama is invaluable for developing a sense of the natural flow and rhythms of language, on a singing pitch that is comfortable to the performer. To announce to your music class that they are going to do some drama can cause some surprise, and usually great pleasure.

Exercises in mime are an excellent starting point. All comment is stilled, attention is concentrated on the movement and pupils quickly lose their self-consciousness.

Arms   Paint a wall; signal to someone a long way away; play a ball game.

Legs   Walk with a limp; as if you are cold; as if on the way to a party; like a pop star coming on stage.

Hands   Knead bread; rub cream into your hands; unscrew a tight lid from a jar; look at your palm and try and tell your fortune; hammer in a nail.

Once pupils have got used to the idea, try giving them some mime to piano accompaniment to help suggest the scene. This need not be elaborate; for example, for the work in pairs, a few rising chords or notes played on the piano, with appropriate feeling as pupils move together, is enough to focus their attention and help them feel in the mood. Then, perhaps some quiet chords for the 'conciliation' a few quick high chords for 'flinching' and a glissando down into a quiet chord for 'collapsing exhausted'.

Look: bored; scared; quietly pleased; pitying; confident; quietly thrilled.

In pairs, move towards each other aggressively. When the music tells you, become conciliatory;

move towards each other in fear. When you meet, flinch away;

move towards each other energetically then collapse, exhausted.

In groups, mime a shipwreck to the appropriate music from *Sheherazade*; mime a gunfight to the gunfight scene from *Billy the Kid*.

Now on to singing. I know of no miraculous way of leading pupils to sing what they say, but I have found that the best exercises which inspire this are those that demand that the pupils *exclaim*. Give some mime exercises such as these:

You are walking to school and your bag bursts open all over the wet road.
You are watching the International Horse Jumping when a horse and rider fall.
You are watching a thriller on television and something goes wrong with your set just at the most exciting moment.

When they have mimed these situations take one of them and discuss what they would say if it really happened. Discourage one-word or two-word ejaculations and encourage complete sentences. Once several people have made realistic suggestions then repeat the exercise, this time asking them to *sing* what they would say. It is a good idea to sing with them so that those who are rather shy can pick up your pitch. Follow this up with several more situations, with little discussion in between, until more and more pupils are singing with confidence. Initial attempts may be very brief, but some pupils will need to have

plucked up a great deal of courage even to sing [music: Oh dear!] However, less

inhibited pupils will usually be most expressive in a short space of time.

This is a version of the first incident suggested above, sung by an 11-year-old:

Arguments

Verbal fluency is usually encouraged by the thought of having an argument! Before doing the following exercises discuss the use of pitch to show emotion.

Also, as pupils are working in pairs, perhaps they want to show, through texture of voice and pitch, the sort of person they are.

Have an argument with your brother or sister as to whose turn it is to . . .
Have a row with your father over the lights that were left on last night when you came home late.
Explain to a policeman why he has found you in a neighbour's garden.

Once they have tried singing an argument, discuss the use of crescendo and accelerando. Emphasize the usefulness of starting slowly and quietly, and then building towards the climax.

A friend has borrowed your best pen. Ask for it back. The friend has lost it and the examinations start tomorrow!
You are gathering courage to go into the swimming pool. A friend keeps teasing and splashing you and, eventually, pushes you in.

Pupils will be quick to suggest possible themes for an argument. This conversation was sung between two pupils about an incident that had just arisen.

At this stage, the argument began to turn into a name-calling session. When the group discussed the work afterwards they came to realize for themselves that this was ineffectual and saw how important it is to have thought out a definite ending, even to a conversation of a few sentences each.

For some time, work is best done with two or three pupils working together. This avoids too much argument, prevents shyer pupils being dominated by others who are more confident, and also means that most of the class will be working with their friends. The ideas you suggest for them to use can be based on everyday situations which will give no problems in thinking out a dialogue. You will be entertained by the variety of scenes that can arise if you suggest that they base their improvisations on a short 'punch line' such as:

Pay attention!	Why on earth are you wearing that!
What a mess!	Keep still! – this could be dangerous!
Don't slam that door!	How many times do I have to tell you . . .
I forgot my homework, Miss.	Only 10p more and I'll be able to . . .
Please Mum, just this once.	You don't really mean it!

Some useful liaison can be done with other departments. What books are the class reading at the moment? What period of history are they studying?

The following conversation was evolved by three pupils who were studying Genesis.

Margaret O'Shea

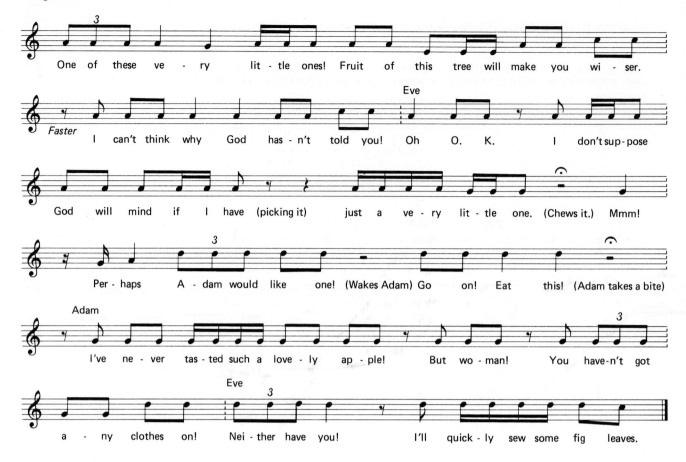

The pupils who were playing the Serpent and Eve were improvising with a beautiful sense of freedom and helped Adam, who was much more shy, to become involved in his short part.

Note the tendency to get stuck at one pitch when improvising both words and melody, and how a new event, such as starting a conversation with a different person, provides the singer with a new impetus.

At this stage pupils may be interested to hear some recorded recitative, such as the conversation between Amahl and his mother when the kings are knocking on the door (*Amahl and the Night Visitors*: Menotti) or some of the witty exchanges in *The Marriage of Figaro*.

Developing a complete scene

Building this improvised work into a group situation is best done by suggesting a scene in which pupils can still work in their small groups, but where they are contributing their improvisation to a composite whole, for example:

A supermarket in which the following events take place: a mother arrives with triplets in a pram and has difficulty in getting past the barrier; a woman has an argument with her husband over whether it is a good idea to buy wine in a supermarket; two lovers walk round dreamily, trying to please each other with what they choose to buy; a pair of shady-looking characters try to use an out-of-date banker's card when making out a cheque and the manager is called; a small child pulls down a display; two people, with full baskets, collide.

An exercise such as this gives very good practice at, one moment, taking the centre of the 'stage', and, next moment, unobtrusively staying in character. There can be plenty of parts also for those who never wish to be in the centre of the stage at all.

Other crowd scenes could be:

On a crowded bus
A group of hitchhikers meeting in a hostel
A protest march (each group with its own slogan)

The school fête
A school assembly
On the beach

The class is now ready to consider some of the following questions before working on a sung scene.

Are you old or young? Distressed or happy? Thoughtful? Boisterous? Man or woman? What difference will this make to the voice you choose to use? Can each of the people in your scene have a very different kind of voice? Do you speak quickly? Hesitantly? Enthusiastically? With an accent? With a rather dull tone? Are you trying to convey an underlying emotion through using the sound of your voice? In each sentence you are singing, is there any word or group of words you would like to emphasize? Will you do this by using a particularly high or low pitch? Will you use more notes for one or more syllables? Is there a type of rhythm that will fit the feeling of your sentence?

Once the connection is made between the pupils' inner hearing and the emotional content of a vocal line they will enjoy trying some scenes which will give them the opportunity of using the full emotional range of their voices. Try suggesting a sequence of contrasting emotions, for example: contentment, shock, fear, tenderness, optimism.

Discuss the sounds of the human voice which may express these emotions, then ask pupils to make up a story which shows this sequence and uses a different type of vocal sound for each section, for example, a whispering thread-like tone for fear. Allow them to scream if necessary!

It is possible to build this type of work into a full-scale production. Pupils who have experienced singing in this way will certainly perform their normal repertoire of songs with a renewed feeling for words. At whatever level you decide to use it, this work means a great deal of fun in the classroom.

Related bibliography

H. Szabo: *The Kodály Concept of Music Education* Boosey & Hawkes, 1969
Three LP records and an accompanying booklet give a musically illustrated guide to a child's musical progress from kindergarten age to an advanced level of attainment.

F. Sandor: *Music Education in Hungary* Boosey & Hawkes, 1969
This book gives an interesting account of music education in Hungarian schools and details the results of research which shows the benefit of having a Kodály-based musical education.

The Kodály Method Boosey & Hawkes
This is a collective title for the 22 books which include exercises, folk songs and original compositions collected or composed by Kodály for use in his Method. They range from the simplicity of the first of the '333 Reading Exercises' to the sophistication of such works as his 'Tricinia – 29 Progressive Three-Part Songs'. The revised English edition is by Geoffrey Russell-Smith.

G. Barnfield: *Creative Drama in Schools* Macmillan, 1968
A guide to how the dramatic possibilities latent in children can be inspired and developed by teachers lacking special training.

Hodgson and Richards: *Improvisation* Methuen, 1966
Suggestions for situations upon which an improvisation may be built.

© Margaret O'Shea

Practical improvisation

Grenville Hancox

Grenville Hancox's philosophy of music education will be shared by many other teachers. He believes that for too many years we have suffered from the idea that music should be seen on the timetable but not heard, and that the music teacher's responsibility to the few could be realized in the dinner-hour:

'While great satisfaction is gained from the performance of music to a tolerable standard by about ten per cent of the school, it can hardly claim to be music in practice. The classroom should be the musical laboratory where learning and discovery take place; where fun is had by pupils, and where the teacher emerges from the lessons sometimes scarred, but always satisfied that he or she is attempting to put music into practice for all children.'

Grenville Hancox's work at Madely Court school has been based around the belief in the need to give children the opportunity to:

1 acquire a skill – no matter how basic
2 recreate music
3 create music
4 sing

In order to do this he believes first that the extensive use of all kinds of musical instruments in the classroom is essential, and secondly that lessons should be organized to give children responsibility:

'Unless they are given the opportunity to take responsibility, they will never show it. If possible, use practice rooms, corridors and spaces outside the class to send children to acquire their skill or invent their piece. Here they will organize, make decisions and co-operate with each other and you.'

The projects which follow have been used in various types of accommodation over the last ten years, and have proved very successful for Grenville Hancox's pupils. They make use of a carefully designed balance of direction and freedom, so that while pupils are encouraged to improvise and create their own music to some extent, there is always a definite musical and educational aim to the ideas.

PROJECT 1

Conductor game

This is a game designed to give children the chance to experiment with a large group of sounds, to acquire experience of handling instruments, and to introduce the concept of notation.

1 Arrange your class in a semi-circle formation and give each child an instrument. (Instruments need not be restricted to pitched/unpitched percussion and orchestral instruments, but can include any sound-producing object from a ruler to a saucepan!) Stringed instruments, if you have them in your school, provide an excellent opportunity for learning correct handling, and for introducing pizzicato technique or glissando effect. Children already learning instruments should be encouraged to play them in the game.
2 Demonstrate the idea of the game to the class. Using a beater or ruler as a baton, instruct the group to play a short loud sound when the beater points in their direction. Absolute silence is required when the baton is in a vertical position. Experiment with your group, ensuring that every player is required to play at least once. Try to create patterns and shapes and contrast the different instrumental timbres.
3 Having played the game for a few minutes, ask for a volunteer to be the new conductor, and during the weeks that you use the game, encourage as many different conductors as possible to direct the activity. Record the results, and listen with the children to the tapes. Discuss them and encourage discrimination in terms of what sounds seem best, or which patterns are most successful.
4 Extend the game with other signals to explore different durations of sound and different dynamic levels. Encourage groupings of instruments and sectional playing at the conductor's request. Find recordings by composers using

groupings of instruments to illustrate contrasts, e.g. Gabrieli's *Sonate pian e forti* or Stockhausen's *Gruppen*.

5 When the group is experienced at this game, introduce the idea of capturing the improvised idea by using a notated score. Using any symbols they choose, ask the group to produce a graphic score of their own piece. Use large sheets of paper for the final presented score.

PROJECT 2

Russian march

1 Organize the classroom before the group enters with pitched percussion, unpitched percussion, and melodic instruments arranged in different areas of the room. Once again, if you have stringed instruments in your school, use them, positioning them in an area well away from the door! Should you have a set of timpani, then pretune to D and A, and to avoid any confusion, tape D E F G A papers on to the keyboard of the classroom piano.

2 Introduce the children to the piece by playing the ostinato part and the melodic row yourself. Improvise on the five-note pattern as one of the children maintains the D – A ostinato with you, and then give the class the same opportunity. All the pitched percussion players should play the ostinato together at first, and any melodic instrument player should play the rising and falling melody on your direction. Encourage the class to play quietly, gradually getting louder and then fading away as the 'army' passes in your and your class's imagination.

You may of course have 80 per cent of your class not knowing correct fingerings on recorders or which strings are D and A on the cello or bass, and who find difficulty in counting up to four. Such a piece is ideal for instruction. I have found children learn it very quickly, and after giving them a little freedom to discover what they are capable of, the piece will come together.

Any pupils who are musically literate can be given the task of adding a suitable part for their instrument, and writing it down prior to improvising with the class.

3 As the piece grows, explore different textures with your class by adding and subtracting the patterns that they have arrived at. Unfortunately the tempo of the march will quicken, and there will be difficulties in keeping it together. Patience will be needed by all!

This project can be developed further by comparing the Russian march to the second movement of Mahler's Symphony No. 1. Some pupils could also be asked to try to make a score of the classroom piece, using the worksheet as a starting point.

Russian March Worksheet

These are the notes we are to use in this piece:

Recorders and flutes etc. play this tune:

Xylophones and violins play this pattern throughout:

Cellos and double basses play this throughout:

Drums can play different rhythms:

Guitars can either strum D minor throughout or pluck the D and A strings of the instrument:

Some further improvisations on the melody notes:

Grenville Hancox

PROJECT 3

The sea

The idea for this project came after a visit to the seaside with a group of children one summer. Among the activities of swimming, football, and ice-cream eating, we listened to the sounds that the sea made. A trip to the seaside with any class of children could provide the opportunity to explore the sounds of these activities. Verbal description, pictures, film, slides, posters, displays in the classroom, can all act as a substitute.

Create an atmosphere in the classroom to be associated with the sea: ask children to bring into class their shells, fishing nets, etc. Consult other staff about work that they might be engaged in that has some bearing upon your project.

The melodic ideas here are more difficult than in the Russian march, but the approach can be similar. The guitar part can be divided among two groups of players, should the technique required initially be too difficult. The ostinati ideas should be introduced gradually to build an increasingly rich texture. Should you have electric amplification, use it to produce the bass ostinato. The melodic idea can be treated as a round, with players entering at 1, 2, or 3, and all those children not playing a wind instrument can produce the vocal sounds 'T's' and 'SH'.

Extension work to this piece is limitless. *The Sea* can be used as the first part of a ternary composition, evoking the sea in a calm mood, progressing towards storm conditions and returning to calm. The storm passages can be improvised or composed by the class or by individuals. Recording sounds on tape and slowing them down to play back can produce evocative sounds reminiscent of the haunting beautiful cries of creatures such as whales. Such improvisations and compositions can be notated and displayed, adding to the materials that you provide in the classroom, based on the sea.

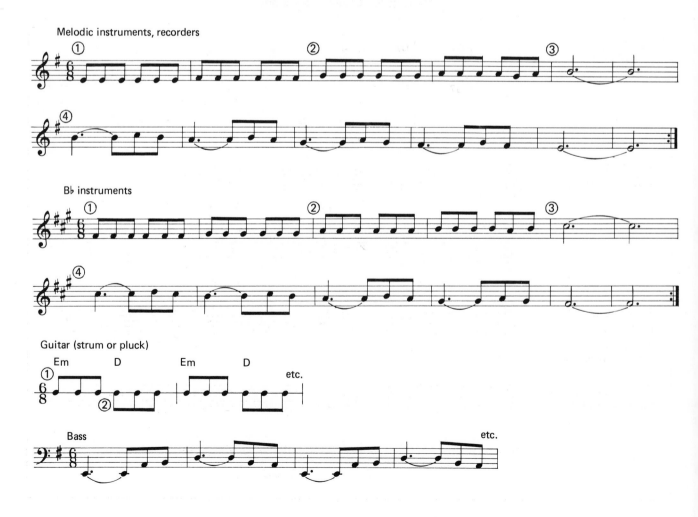

PROJECT 4

Pentatonic blues

As with a lot of good music, the simplest ideas tend to be the best ones. The blues offers a platform for improvisation, so try to encourage simplicity in the creation of the music. If a blues sequence in D is used (in whatever formula), a pentatonic row of F G A C D can be used as a basis for the beginning of improvisation.

Remove the offending notes E and B from xylophones and experiment yourself at playing an improvisation over the blues sequence. Using beaters, try to improvise in lengths of four bar phrases (a *riff*) so that the phrase appears three times in the space of the 12 bars. Having done this, pass the idea on to your class.

Arrange the instruments in sections once again. Access to stringed instruments means that open strings can provide the root notes of the sequence, even if there are no guitars available. For guitarists, the chords of D, G and A will be learned very quickly by some children, while others will take longer, and so if necessary the chords can be divided amongst the players (i.e. one group plays D when required, and so on). The melodic instruments can at first play the associated chord notes with the guitar/string players, so that the whole class becomes familiar with the pattern being used.

At first, confidence will need to be established, so allow the class chance to improvise together, and then ask each pupil in turn to improvise. Encourage every player at this stage, demanding more and more from the group as time goes on. The Pentatonic Blues idea can be extended to great lengths: word setting, historical research, instrumental techniques, etc.

Pentatonic Blues Worksheet

Early music

Michael Burnett

Many music teachers will be conscious of what may appear to be a 'bandwagon' of early or medieval music in schools, where consorts of viols perform in school concerts and sixth form madrigal groups rehearse in the lunch-hour. Although early music enthusiasts abound, the presumed esoteric nature of this type of music still deters many teachers from experimenting with it.

In this chapter Michael Burnett shows how early music can not only be brought into schools which cannot afford facsimile instruments, but can be used with pupils whose musical experience is comparatively limited. At the same time, the practical projects he describes allow flexibility for a fairly wide range of musical ability, while the somewhat abstract but very enjoyable nature of this style could also bring together pupils of all ages.

In one sense, though, early music in schools does pose a problem. On the one hand scholars have unearthed a large quantity of material which, due to its inherent simplicity of melody and form, is suitable for use in the classroom. On the other hand the classroom situation does not lend itself readily to the achievement of stylistic integrity, a matter rightly of concern to the early music specialist. Michael Burnett is quite clear about what we should do:

> *'Should we leave early music to the scholars and history books? Or should we bring it into the classroom, fully aware that classroom performances will result in stylistic compromise? I believe that teachers in general are people who believe in doing something rather than nothing and accordingly advocate the latter course. Better that our music classes experience early music at first hand than that this wealth of music should remain on the musicologist's shelves or solely in the repertoire of the specialist performer.'*

For the purposes of this chapter Michael Burnett has taken early music to include music from 1100–1600, a period embracing the songs of the troubadours, the rise of polyphony and the Renaissance. From this wealth of music he has selected a variety of examples which lend themselves to classroom performance. These projects are preceded by some information on instrumentation and followed by suggestions for listening to early music.

Instrumentation

Medieval shawms

Where parallels can be drawn between modern school instruments and those in use in early music, these can help justify the use of the former in the classroom performance of early music. In other cases it is possible to establish some general links in terms of tone colour between a modern instrument and one which was in use during the period 1100–1600. Bearing these factors in mind, it may well prove possible to set up a classroom ensemble which has some resemblance in overall tone colour to that of, say, a medieval band. This seems to me to be a reasonable aim, although the realities of the classroom may well prove frustrating. The following suggestions as to classroom equivalents for early instruments are therefore made with the proviso that where the instruments mentioned are not available others should be substituted.

Wind instruments

The raucous sounds of reed instruments such as the shawm were perhaps the most thrilling of early instrument timbres. The present-day bombarde (used, for example, by the Breton folk musician Alan Stivell) is a contemporary equivalent and is not too expensive to buy. But the classroom melodica has an abrasive quality which makes it an adequate substitute for a shawm in the school ensemble.

Of non-reed instruments it is the recorder which has a family tree extending back into the Middle Ages. Although now mass-produced in plastic, the modern recorder is essentially the same instrument as the medieval one, and as such it should play a leading role in the making of early music in the classroom. Schools fortunate enough to possess other members of the family besides the ubiquitous descant should certainly also incorporate these instruments in the music-making.

Percussion instruments

Instruments commonly found in the classroom such as castanets, cymbals, tambourines and triangles all have almost exact early music equivalents. Similarly, various sizes and types of drum can be used in the classroom ensemble, on the basis that they have early parallels. The small classroom tom-tom, for example, has a sound similar to the medieval tabor, while school-made shakers and drums can also be used.

Tuned percussion instruments should be incorporated in the ensemble if your school is fortunate enough to have them. Glockenspiels, metallophones and chime bars have similar sound characteristics to medieval bells, while the xylophone has an ancient history, and its incisive sounds can help give definition to the classroom ensemble.

Keyboard instruments

Exact modern equivalents of early instruments are not common, although a number of harpsichord kits are available which might in the long-term prove viable projects for a school with an enterprising craft department. A number of schools possess small electronic organs which can produce reedy tone-colours somewhat reminiscent of the regal. Failing an organ, a piano will have to be used in cases where a keyboard instrument is essential, although this will certainly cause displeasure among purists!

String instruments

The modern acoustic guitar has early music relatives and would prove an asset in the classroom ensemble. Chordal dulcimers, where available, should also be used as their sound quality is not unlike that of the medieval psaltery and dulcimer. In schools where violin lessons are provided, beginners on this instrument should be encouraged to play in the ensemble. The early viol (which, by the way, is *not* the ancestor of the violin) had a thin and rather precise tone colour. This is best simulated by young violinists who should avoid vibrato and keep to first position.

Brass instruments

Modern trumpets and trombones are related to early trumpets and sackbuts, although their tone is mellower and they are much more versatile. Should you be lucky enough to have beginners on trumpet and trombone in your class, then certainly these instruments should be incorporated in the ensemble when the music has the right sort of martial flavour.

PROJECT 1

Veni Sancte Spiritus

This 17th-century sequence melody is best played on recorders. It should be taken slowly and easily. Once the tune has been learned, the percussion parts may be added, played by a second group of students. The melody may be repeated a number of times with varied instrumentation to form a longer piece. Here is a plan of one possible version:

Introduction	triangle ostinato played twice
Verse 1	two recorders accompanied by triangle
Link	tambourine ostinato played twice
Verse 2	all the recorders accompanied by tambourine
Link	triangle ostinato played twice
Verse 3	all the recorders accompanied by triangle and drum

(Substitute melodicas for recorders throughout if necessary.)

PROJECT 2

Song of the ass

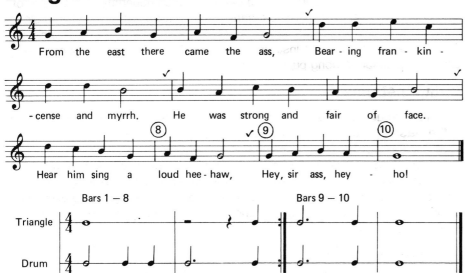

This famous tune is an example of a conductus or melody composed for use in a ceremonial procession. In this case the procession formed part of a play during which a girl, representing the Virgin, rode into the cathedral at Beauvais on an ass. With younger students the melody could perhaps be sung, and words are included for this purpose. In the case of older students I suggest that the tune should be played on melodicas or recorders. (If there are any violinists in the class then they should join in too.) Parts for triangle and drum are included and, again, I suggest that once all the parts have been learned the tune could be repeated a number of times with varied instrumentation, this according to the resources at your disposal.

PROJECT 3

L'homme armé

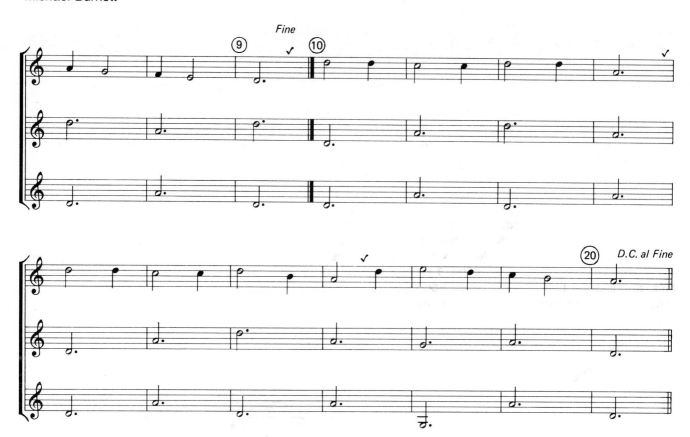

A popular French folk-song, this melody was incorporated in many Mass compositions of the 15th and 16th centuries. For classroom purposes I suggest that the tune should be played on recorders and/or melodicas. I have added an accompaniment which would best suit tuned percussion instruments with sustaining power, such as metallophones or glockenspiels. If necessary this could, of course, also be played on recorders and melodicas. Accompaniment 2 is designed for beginner violinists to play on open strings. The untuned accompaniments are for tambourine and drum. Here is a plan of one possible performing version of the tune:

Verse 1 recorders/melodicas play tune, accompanied in bars 1–9 by tambourine and 10–20 by drum

Verse 2 melodicas play tune, accompanied by metallophones/glockenspiels

Verse 3 recorders play bars 1–9 of tune, accompanied by tambourine; melodicas, bars 10–20 accompanied by drum. All instruments join in for repeat of bars 1–9

PROJECT 4

Hymn to St Magnus

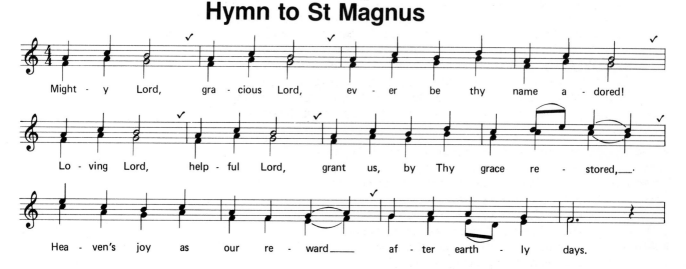

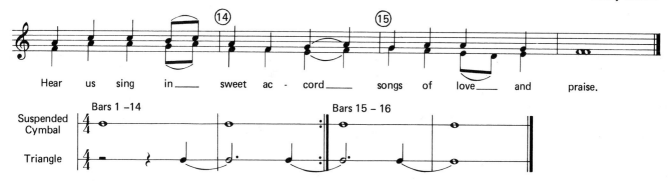

This 12th-century hymn is an early example of organum in thirds, and stems from
Scotland. (St Magnus is the patron saint of the Orkney Islands.) As it stands, the
hymn is immediately practicable for classroom use. It may be sung or played on
recorders, melodicas or any other available melody instruments. Parts for triangle
and tambourine are also suggested. The piece would prove particularly effective
if it were performed chorally the first time through, with recorders the second
time, and finally with instruments and voices together. The triangle could enter
with recorders and tambourine in the last verse.

PROJECT 5

Qui creavit coelum

This hymn comes from a 15th-century processional of Benedictine nuns in
Chester. The simple tune and refrains 'Lully, lully, lu' and 'By-by, by-by, by'
suggest its popular origins. I suggest that the tune should first of all be played
by recorders and/or melodicas. It should be taken quite slowly, with breathing
marks observed. Once learned, the tune may be accompanied by one or both
of the ostinato patterns for triangle and shaker. In order to differentiate between
verse and refrain, the latter could be played louder by both recorders and
percussion. Alternatively, a number of the instruments could be silent during
the verse section and join in for the refrain. With younger classes the tune
could also be sung and some words are included for this purpose. Finally, a
variety of different versions of the tune could be played one after the other to
make a longer piece. Here is one way of putting the components together:

Introduction triangle ostinato played twice
Verse 1 recorders (refrain louder) accompanied by triangle
Link shaker ostinato played twice
Verse 2 voices (refrain louder) accompanied by shaker
Link triangle ostinato played twice
Verse 3 melodicas (refrain louder) accompanied by triangle
Link triangle and shaker ostinati played twice
Verse 4 recorders and voices (melodicas join in for refrain)
accompanied by triangle and shaker

45

Michael Burnett

Dance

Woodblock

Drum

I have included the first 14 bars only of this lively 14th-century dance from Italy. It should be played on any melody instruments which happen to be available and needs to be taken at a steady rather than fast pace. Simple parts for drum and woodblock are included, and these may serve as introductions to, or interludes between, repetitions of the dance.

Innsbruck

Ostinati (untuned perc.)

Last bar

This tune forms a particularly effective contrast with the previous dance. It is by the 15th-century composer Heinrich Isaac and the original words tell of his sorrow at leaving the city of Innsbruck for foreign parts. In the version below I have taken the liberty of reducing the original four parts to two. I suggest that these should be played on recorders and/or melodicas beginning with the tune. Once this has been learned then one or more of the ostinato patterns for untuned percussion can be added and the second tuned part put in if practicable. As before, the song could be played through a number of times with varied instrumentation.

PROJECT 8

Summer is a-coming in

* C♯ in original

Summer is a-coming in is the most famous of all English medieval compositions. It dates from the last half of the 13th century and is particularly suitable for use in today's classroom because of its liveliness and adaptability. The tune may be both sung and played. It can be treated as a two-, three- or four-part round and it has two simple tuned ostinato accompaniments (slightly simplified here) which may be added if desired. For singing purposes I have included a rough translation, which delicately omits the original reference to the bowel movements of the medieval buck. Here is a plan of one possible way of presenting the piece, using voices and a variety of the instruments mentioned earlier:

Introduction	Ostinato 1 played twice by melodicas, glockenspiels and xylophones joining in the second time with Ostinato 2
Verse 1	recorders play tune with ostinati accompaniment allocated as above
Link	ostinati continue twice with piano or organ joining in with melodicas 8vo and violin joining in with glockenspiels and xylophones
Verse 2	voices join in with recorders, ostinati continue as allocated above
Link	untuned ostinati join in with tuned ostinati played twice
Verse 3	recorders and tuned ostinati stop, voices divided into two groups treat the melody as a round accompanied by untuned ostinati
Link	tuned ostinati join in with untuned ostinati (instrumentation as allocated above) played twice. (Add trombone on Ostinato 1 8vo and trumpet on Ostinato 2 if available.)
Verse 4	all ostinati continue, recorders join with voices on the tune

Listening to early music

The range of available recordings of early music is now considerable, and the sounds of early instruments in modern facsimile can be brought into the classroom with ease. However, ease of access to recordings of early music brings with it dangers of which we are already well aware in relation to the music of later periods. Only a relatively small proportion of the recorded material is suitable for the 11–14 age range, and I have a nightmare vision of classes of 13-year olds listening to Masses by Ockeghem and Dunstable, just as in the past they listened to symphonies by Beethoven and Brahms.

In order to ensure that listening to early music is an active rather than passive lesson, it is essential to choose music which is short (or can effectively be shortened), which makes use of incisive instrumental colours and which is clear-cut in terms of melody and form. Given these factors then the teacher is in the position to direct the listening of the class, and to turn 'musical appreciation' into a subject for active minds. Each piece of music should be selected on the basis that it clearly demonstrates certain specific musical elements upon which the students' minds may beneficially be focused.

A further danger inherent in early music recordings is that, as in the case of other periods, it is all too easy in using the recordings to imply a separation between *listening* and *doing*, as if there were one kind of music played on a gramophone and another played in the classroom. It is therefore important in choosing listening music to select material which, in one way or another, can be made to come alive through practical experience during the lesson. For example, one piece of early music may have a predominant rhythm which can be demonstrated and then played by students. Another may have a tune which can be played on classroom instruments. (A list of recordings, where available, of the pieces mentioned in Projects 1–8 is included in the *Resources* section of this chapter.) Yet another early piece may make use of a tuned ostinato which can similarly be demonstrated and imitated in the classroom.

Here are some examples of music suitable for classroom listening. The pieces are taken from the first four albums mentioned under **Records** in the **Resources** section of this chapter.

composer	title	listening points	album no.
Nicholson	The Jew's Dance	use of recorder and lute	1
Susato	Six Dances	use of a wide variety of early instruments; contrasts of style; form	1
Anon	Danse Royale	use of shawm and 2 tabors; tabor rhythms as basis of class rhythm collage	2
Anon	Piper's Fancy	use of pipe and tabor; tabor rhythm as basis of class rhythm collage	2
Anon	El Pomo	use of harpsichord; predominant rhythm as basis of class rhythm collage	3
Anon	La Rocha	use of recorder, viol, fiddle, and harpsichord	3
Moderne, attr.	Pavana la Bataille	use of trumpets, sackbuts and kettledrums; martial rhythms	4
Anon	S'Maidlein	use of consort of recorders	4

Related Resources

Music for use in the classroom

A. and M. Bagenal (arr): *This Merry Company* (Parts 1 and 2) OUP, 1980/81
    Although this publication is designed for primary schools it contains a useful selection of music, all of which is recorded on cassette

F. Baines (arr): *Dances from the Middle Ages* Schott, 1965
    Five pieces arranged for recorder with a suggested drum part

M. Burnett (arr): *A Feast of Music* Chappell, 1976
    Seven medieval dances and hymns arranged for recorders, tuned and untuned percussion

R. McGrady (arr): *Four 13th-century Pieces* Chester, 1973
    Arrangements for recorders

B. Sargent (ed): *Minstrels* and *Troubadours* CUP, 1974
    These two books contain a wide selection of material.
    Simple ostinato accompaniments are included

Other useful sources of music

T. Dart (ed): *Invitation to Medieval Music* (4 vols) Stainer & Bell, 1967
A. Davison and W. Apel (eds): *Historical Anthology of Music, Vol 1* Harvard, 1976

Records

1 *Two Renaissance Dance Bands* HMV HQS 1249
2 *Music of the Crusades* Argo ZRG 673
3 *The Pleasures of the Royal Courts* Nonesuch H-71326
4 *The Instruments of the Middle Ages and Renaissance* Vanguard VSD 71219/20

5 *Music of 14th-century Florence* Argo ZRG 642
6 *Instruments of the Middle Ages and Renaissance* HMV SLS 988
This two-record set accompanies the book with the same title by David
Munrow, published by Oxford University Press

Recordings of pieces mentioned in the projects

Song of the ass Pye GSGC 14092
L'homme armé Philips SAL 3722
Hymn to St Magnus Supraphon SUA 10741
Innsbruck Argo ZRG 728
Summer is a-coming in Enigma K 53571

Articles and school textbooks

'Early Music for Everyone', *Music Stand*, Vol 3, 1976
'A Feast of Music', *Music Teacher*, Nov. 1976
J. Arnold: Oxford Topics in Music *Medieval Music* OUP, 1982
An informative, illustrated introduction to the subject with lots of practical
projects.

The *Early Music Shops* in London and Bradford stock a range of modern
facsimiles of early instruments, some of which (bombardes, panpipes, three-
holed pipes, tabors) are relatively inexpensive. They can also supply a number of
instrumental kits. The addresses of the shops are:

47 Chiltern Street
London
W1M 1HN
tel: 01-935 1242

28 Sunbridge Road
Bradford
BD1 2AE
tel: 0274 393753

© Michael Burnett

The uses of pop

Tony Attwood

Although Keith Swanwick's seminal work Pop Music and the Teacher *appeared in 1968, little attention was paid to the use of pop music in schools for the next eight years. While after-school youth clubs may have sported the occasional school group, music teachers never considered using pop music in any serious sense in the classroom.*

But by the 1970s the teenagers of the 1960s were themselves music teachers. They had lived their teens through a time of intense development of pop music, most notable for the rise of The Beatles, and entered secondary classrooms with hundreds of melodies still in their heads. This was a decade which had begun with Michael Young's influential book Knowledge and Control, *which dared to question the established curriculum, not to mention Paynter and Aston's* Sound and Silence *and Brian Dennis's* Experimental Music in Schools.

In 1976 Pop Music in School *was published, which contained a variety of arguments for and examples of the possibilities of using pop music in music teaching. In the same year the first CSE course and examination in pop music was established at Holland Park school, with a good deal of unexpected attendant publicity. Tony Attwood had played a leading part in advising Holland Park and other schools on how to develop the use of pop in music teaching, and during the next three years was involved in producing the first published materials on pop for use in schools.*

This chapter is a general resumé of the various uses of pop in secondary schools, and covers the essential areas of practical work, 'theory', history and learning about the pop industry. For those who wish to go into a particular area in more detail there is a comprehensive resource section at the end of the chapter.

Practical work

Playing pop and rock instruments

As every teacher must be aware, the cost and noise levels of pop and rock instruments make them difficult to use in the normal school situation. However, where pupils and students have their own equipment, and where the school can provide one or two items (such as an extra amplifier and microphone) playing pop music on the instruments for which it was written may feature as a small group activity after school or during certain 'option' periods. Where it does it will certainly be of interest to many pupils aged 13 and upwards.

The following general instructions are for work with a group of performers who have some ability in playing instruments but little experience of playing in a group.

The first move by the teacher must be to get the group to play, no matter what the shortcomings (supposed or real) of the instruments available. A good introduction is always a twelve-bar blues, which also serves to cut short any dispute as to what songs the group should be playing. The melody used is unimportant; what is vital is the agreed chord structure of the blues, which allows the group to get used to playing together. The repeated sequence (in E major) is given below with each chord taking up one bar:

E E E E; A A E E; B7 A E B7 :‖

After the group has started to work together lead lines can be introduced on guitar or keyboard. In order to help out with this stage of the development the teacher may wish to play a simple accompaniment on the piano. This should be built around a string of chords with the third omitted and the seventh added. With the use of these devices and a lot of patience the group should begin to function together rather than as a string of individuals. (Examples of Blues lead lines, riffs and accompaniments will be found on pages 10 to 13.)

The group will of course wish to move on to some known pop and rock songs, or into their own preferred style, as soon as possible. The teacher's role here is clearly to find out what items the pupils want to play and (probably just through listening to the borrowed record) to prepare chord and lyrics sheets. Having organized the music in this way, the next task is to introduce the group to the idea of practising one piece several times, though they may find the whole concept of disciplined rehearsals somewhat different from their image of how the pop world operates!

After a number of songs have been mastered, and when technique is improving, the pupils can be encouraged to write their own songs. Generally there are three ways forward; via the pupil who writes lyrics only, the pupil who dreams up melodies and the pupil who improvises original chord sequences. Each of these can become an introduction to a song-writing session, and this can allow the teacher to expand the activities of the group to a wider range of pupils in the school, with requests to pupils to help write a song for a school group.

Singing pop and rock in class

Many teachers find that singing has a part to play in school music lessons with pupils up to the age of 13 or 14. The advantage of singing pop songs in school is simply that, because the songs are identifiable by the pupils as 'their' music, they are likely to join in and sing with more enthusiasm. Furthermore, for those pupils who are learning to play pop guitar (or who are teaching themselves to play pop piano) the songs used in the singing class can be of use instrumentally.

Teachers have a choice of three sources of music: current favourites drawn from the top 50 charts, lesser known (or even unknown) songs which are in the pop style and past favourites from the pop repertoire.

The problem with current pop favourites is that many of them are not appropriate for class or school singing; teachers may find some lyrics unacceptable, melodies may either be too restricted or too wide ranging for most pupils to handle (as with the excessive use of falsetto), or they may not be easily arranged for accompaniment by piano or guitar. Thus if current hits are to be used it is essential for the teacher to make the choice rather than for the pupils to be asked to make a selection. (Normally about 25 per cent of the records in the top 50 at any one time are usable in the class, although it is often difficult to obtain accurate copies of the printed music, and teachers should be prepared to transcribe from the record.)

For a guide to the current top selling records teachers should listen either to the Radio 1 chart broadcast in full once a week (currently on Sunday evenings) or the local charts broadcast by most commercial radio stations, again usually on Sundays.

It is often assumed that pupils only want to sing the current chart successes, but this is certainly not true. In general, enthusiasm is shown for all music within the pop style with lyrics that relate to matters that concern the pupils themselves. Thus lesser known songs may be taken from pop LPs, or can be found on past hits. Pupils will often lend copies of albums to teachers to enable them to search for suitable tracks.

Apart from playing through old hits the teacher may also find anthologies of sheet music helpful in the search for suitable songs. The best known and most widely used anthologies in schools are those of the songs of Paul Simon, the Beatles, and Elvis Presley. Such volumes can keep the teacher supplied with suitable songs for several terms. (See bibliography for further resource suggestions.)

Using improvised instruments

The tea-chest, the tin can, the large beer can, the comb and paper . . . all have been used successfully in the classroom to accompany a melody or chord sequence being played on piano or guitar. In a sense, such improvision lies at the very heart of musical activity in the pop world, and although recorded pop has lost much of its improvisatory origins, it is never far away in the 'live' concert.

For this sort of improvisation an initial collection of items needs to be made; indeed anything that makes a sound and which can be brought into the classroom is acceptable here. The class can listen to and discuss the use of each item, from yoghurt pots filled with sand to sheets of metal shaken to sound like thunder.

Such a collection can obviously lead to a free-flowing improvisation, in the 'creative' style, but may also be used in pop, with the teacher playing a repeated pop, reggae or disco rhythm on the piano and the pupils improvising their rhythmic accompaniment. A typical rhythm for the piano in reggae style is illustrated below:

Following this a melody can be improvised over the top of the rhythm, again with a piano lead, and the melodic instruments can be brought in.

Through this process of allowing pupils to collect their own sound sources and experiment with them, teachers often find that the responsiveness of pupils to the sounds they make in the improvisation is greatly enhanced, especially when a solid chord sequence is added at the piano (such as a repeating D major, C major, G major, D major sequence with two bars of each chord). Sometimes a sense of adventure needs to be stimulated to stop everyone simply beating out the four beats of the bar; for example, by showing how helpful the addition of a quaver or semiquaver beat at the end of a bar can be.

Using classroom instruments to play pop

The major problem of using classroom instruments in the performance of pop songs is that pupils can feel they are not doing the 'real thing'; in other words they are somehow demeaning their own music by playing it on glockenspiels rather than on electric guitars. For this reason it is often better to avoid the current chart successes and turn to past hits from the pop repertoire, to folk-songs arranged with pop-style chords, to songs written by the class, and improvisations based around chord sequences.

As already mentioned, the twelve-bar blues is often a good starting point, and can be adapted to the instruments available. Thus glockenspiels and xylophones can be allocated to pupils with each pupil playing just one note of each chord as follows:

Chord	E	A	B7
Glock 1	E	E	D sharp
Glock 2	G sharp	A	A
Glock 3	B	A	B
Glock 4	E	C sharp	F sharp

Gradually these static parts can be developed and improvised into four melodies, rather in the style of traditional jazz. At the same time, those pupils who are learning orchestral instruments can also use their abilities by taking on parts based around the chords. New chord sequences can also be evolved according to the instrumentation available; for example, a sequence involving a flattened seventh chord (such as D major in the key of E) is well suited to performance with violins that can only play safely on open strings. Further discussion of the use of chord sequences is given on page 57 under *Pop as an approach to chordal awareness*. (See bibliography for further Blues resources.)

Learning pop guitar in the classroom

The essential prerequisite for this scheme is a set of acoustic guitars, with enough instruments so that each member of the class need share with only one other person. The next step is to find out a) who can play the guitar (however imperfectly) so that players can be seated with someone of approximately the same ability, and b) who is left-handed, so that these people can share guitars strung especially for them.

From this point each pair of pupils has a guitar and set of notes (with guitar 'windows') demonstrating how to play a few chords. Where most of the class is at the same standard the teacher can introduce each new instruction sheet with explanations, hints on fingering and so on. This is especially important at the start where the newcomers to the guitar need the concept of the 'windows' explained to them. The pupils then try and pick out the chords shown, whilst the teacher tours the class. Every few minutes the pairs of pupils swop the guitar over, with the person not playing now listening and helping.

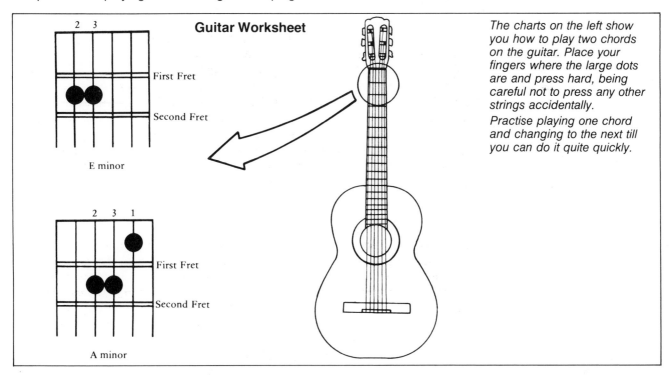

Guitar Worksheet

First Fret

Second Fret

E minor

First Fret

Second Fret

A minor

The charts on the left show you how to play two chords on the guitar. Place your fingers where the large dots are and press hard, being careful not to press any other strings accidentally.

Practise playing one chord and changing to the next till you can do it quite quickly.

After two half-hour sessions most pupils will be able to play three chords (even if very hesitantly) and the teacher can develop the lessons by introducing songs which just use those chords, and which the pupils can sing in their pairs. It may be best to start with a nursery rhyme, such as *Old Macdonald* (in A major), and then move on to some suitable pop songs. The chords of A minor and E minor are also very easy to start with. Even if the speed of chord changes needed in the songs is beyond the capability of the pupils, these should still be introduced early on, as pupils gain much benefit from recognizing that even the little they know (that is, three or four chords) will be enough to play certain songs which they like, as long as they practise.

Teachers considering this approach to learning the guitar are often worried by two points. Firstly, the sound of around 15 guitars being played simultaneously may be thought to be distracting to the pupils, though in fact they do not find it so. Secondly, there is the question of learning an instrument without practising at home. Obviously home practice is ideal, but where this is not possible pupils can often do some work at school in the lunch break, or after school. Even where no extra time is given to practising there is still rapid progress made in class. Furthermore, it may be noted that an acoustic guitar remains one of the most popular presents for 13- and 14-year-olds, and where parents have been involved in buying a present they often take a direct interest in the pupil's progress on it.

Some final thoughts

It is important that the guitars used should be folk guitars and not classical guitars, which have wider necks. It is also important that no attempt is made (at least in the early lessons) to introduce conventional notation, for this slows down the speed at which pupils come to play accompaniments to known pop songs. Similarly, melodies can also be introduced later.

Using the keyboard as a pop instrument

There are two approaches to using the keyboard as a pop instrument: one is predominantly chordal, and the other melodic. My experience has been that for most pupils the approach which leads from chords *into* melodies is by far the best.

Unfortunately it is often difficult to arrange such lessons simply because there are 30 pupils in the class and only one piano. A small inroad into this problem can be made with the use of three pupils together to play chords at the piano while the rest of the class play improvised or classroom instruments, as described earlier.

With this system one pupil may play the bass notes of the chords in the chord sequences, whilst the others play between them the chords in root position or first inversion. If the pupils already have experience at playing parts of chords on glocks or xylophones then the approach will seem quite familiar and reasonable to them. This method is particularly useful if one is playing reggae with its continuing emphasis on the off beats of each bar. The following rhythm can then be utilized:

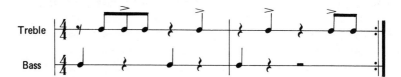

Once pupils are used to this very simple form of work they can progress to playing chords in root positions themselves, and once C major has been mastered it is easy to play D minor, E minor, F major and so on. After this the enthusiastic pupil is quite likely to discover, through listening, the way to amend A minor into D major and further experimentation can lead on to other chords being discovered. It is from this point that pupils can progress to simple 'runs' on the piano which are so much a part of pop and rock music. Again the pupil who has been through a system of learning about chords first will almost certainly be interested in devising his or her own runs. A typical example of a run played against a chord of C major is:

Theory through pop

Using pop music to teach notation

For some pupils the task of coming to terms with traditional notation is made harder because it does not seem to directly relate to the music that they listen to in their spare time. For the complete beginner, the learning of the fundamentals of notational theory can be made more exciting by drawing examples from the world of popular music. For the more advanced student, the teacher's careful selection of printed music drawn from the world of pop can even help with score reading.

For the complete beginner the teacher should introduce extracts from pieces with which the pupils are to some degree familiar. Having played extracts from the music (either on a record or on the piano) the teacher should show the pupils extracts from the printed score, drawing attention to various features revealed in it. In the extract below, from the Elvis Presley hit *It's Now or Never*, the first eight bars can be used to illustrate the question of key signatures, ties, dotted rhythms, rests and so on.

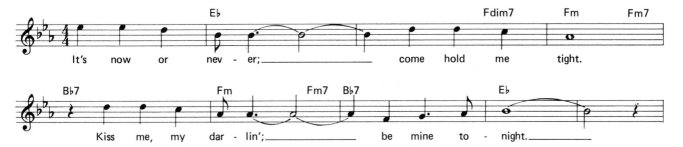

After this procedure has been repeated several times with different songs, the order of presentation may be reversed. Pupils could be shown an extract from a song (without words) *before* hearing it, so that they may try to judge the sound of the piece first. The more advanced pupil should be able to cope with a melody plus the normal piano accompaniment, and should be able to recognize well-known melodies from seeing the score.

Pop as an approach to chordal awareness

It is interesting to note that whereas many teenagers who have taught themselves to play pop guitar show a very highly developed sense of chordal awareness (so that after hearing a chord sequence once or twice they can usually write down what they have heard) many students at music college who have been conventionally trained find this very much more difficult.

Being able to determine the exact nature of a chord sequence is a very valuable attribute for a musician. It is certainly a benefit for anyone taking the aural examination in an O or A level course, where the ability to make rapid shorthand notes about the chord structure of a piece of two- or four-part music can help the student to write down the full score more accurately.

Mention has already been made of the twelve-bar blues with its standard three-chord structure, and if at all possible teachers should make arrangements for pupils to play some twelve-bar blues (in several keys) on guitars, classroom instruments and anything else available as an introduction to the topic of chordal awareness. (See page 57 for suggestions.) Once the pupils are well versed in playing and listening to the twelve-bar blues some other chords can be added and new sequences invented, such as:

C	Am	F	G	
A	Dm	Em	F	G
Dm7	Dm7	Cm7	Cm7	

(This is a particular favourite in much disco music.)

After introducing such sequences the teacher can develop chordal awareness further by using pop songs already known to the pupils. It is helpful for the performers to see a copy of the lyrics of the song with the chords written in above or below the lyrics. If their own parts are then added to this bare outline they will begin to see how their own music fits in to the basic chordal structure.

Having established the above procedure, the students' developing awareness can be tested by playing sequences from known songs on the piano and asking the pupils to write these down. Later, completely unknown sequences can be introduced.

Musical forms in pop

Although most pop songs appear in one of a very limited number of musical forms, it is still possible to make use of these structures when introducing pupils to the often difficult concept of musical form.

The basic pop song is strophic, with chorus and verse alternating, and the teacher should first find a few examples of this from recent pop records and play extracts to the pupils. To ensure that everyone understands the difference between verse and chorus, the teacher might ask the pupils to mark down the number of choruses and verses that appear, and the occasional repeated chorus may catch a few unwary pupils out! The pupils may then be encouraged to write their own pieces in this style, perhaps just writing the words at first.

Ternary form is also used in pop, with what musicians call the 'middle 8' (even when it is not eight bars long) as section B. Sometimes the songs are made slightly more complicated by the introduction of a chorus and the playing of the verse once as an instrumental. A pop ternary piece including these devices could look like this:

Verse 1
Chorus
Verse 2
Chorus
Middle 8
Verse 3
Chorus
Instrumental verse
Middle 8
Verse 3
Chorus
Chorus

Songs in other forms are rarely found in the charts, although they do appear from time to time. However, LPs made by groups in the more progressive pop fields often do branch out into more varied forms, and it is worth while inviting older pupils to listen carefully to their albums in the hope of finding one or two pieces of music that are in alternative styles.

Finally, there are also pop music cycles, which are often called 'concept albums' or 'pop operas'. The most famous of these is *Tommy*, by The Who, while the best known through-composed piece is *Tubular Bells* by Mike Oldfield. Both types of work offer new insights into musical form and can be effectively presented to older pupils for analysis.

Miscellaneous work with pop

The history of pop

New paperback volumes claiming to be complete histories of pop music are published regularly, and it is well worth keeping a small selection, so that those pupils who elect to write a selective history of the subject have some raw material to work from in the school library. Compilation albums containing selections of hits from the past are also issued frequently, and teachers should be concerned that pupils doing such projects have a chance to listen to the hits from previous years. Several volumes have also been published which list top selling LPs and singles since the early 1950s, which are updated regularly, and *The New Musical Express* publishes charts each week from previous years, along with the current lists of top selling records.

The use of pop songs from the past in comparison with current hits is undoubtedly difficult, and many teachers have found it impossible to move pupils beyond comments that the oldies were either 'quite nice' or 'stupid and boring'. Stylistic comparisons often seem beyond many pupils, presumably because of the immediacy of the current hit records. However, for the teacher who is prepared to spend time collecting information and records on one particular period, an interesting set of lessons can be evolved by considering one particular three- or four-year span from both a musical and social perspective. The pupils can be given information about the concerns of young people at that time, about the major events, the popular 'human interest' stories, the sport, and the pop music news. From all this, and from listening to the top records of the time, the pupils should gain a 'feel' for the period. Only after this has been obtained should the teacher attempt to make comparisons with today, firstly in social terms and then in musical terms. Some teachers appear to enter this field with the mistaken view that pop music from one era sounds much the same as that from another. In fact pop seems to go through a predictable series of phases, and quite often one phase is a reaction against the previous style. (See Resources, page 60, for further resource suggestions.)

The music industry

Many teachers now accept the obvious benefit of helping pupils to understand just how the music industry operates, and fortunately in recent years the industry has shown itself willing to explain its activities to pupils and teachers.

There are two main areas that can be studied:

Radio

Local commercial radio is expanding rapidly at the moment, and it is clear that by the end of the 80s over 90 per cent of the population will be served by at least one commercial station. Although few stations have the space which enables school parties to be shown round they will usually respond to requests for information about the station and how it selects the records it plays. This may be the responsibility of a Head of Music, of the Senior Presenter, or in the case of small stations the Programme Controller.

Record companies

Most record companies are located in London, and only a few of these are willing to co-operate with schools in educational ventures. However, a small number of books have recently appeared that do go some way to explaining how groups get record contracts, how records are made, and so on.

The experience of music: projects for older pupils

Most music in Britain is experienced via the radio. After that in popularity comes the record player, and a long way behind that comes the live performance.

Many pupils are obviously interested in the statistics of musical success, as can be seen from the way that pop charts on the radio and in newspapers are avidly studied and commented upon. If a teenager knows anything about pop music it is what is currently in the top 10. In order to develop this line of interest and use it in school the music teacher may feel inclined to link up with the social studies teacher to produce projects for older students.

Radio

All independent local radio stations subscribe to a scheme known as JICRAR, which produces a very detailed analysis of who listens to what on commercial radio. Each report costs over £100 to purchase, but fortunately some elements from the statistics are extracted and occasionally published separately. (Details can be obtained from the Association of Independent Radio Contractors, 8 Great James St., London WC1, tel. 01-405 5036.) The BBC publish their own figures which are given in summary in an annual survey available from BBC publications, and the other commercial stations (such as Manx Radio and Radio Luxembourg) also publish their own data.

What is of interest to many pupils is the listenership in the area around the school, and the local commercial radio station may be persuaded to supply their figures from the latest JICRAR survey. Pupils can then check those figures through a questionnaire administered locally which asks these questions:
 a Which of the following radio stations have you listened to at least once in the past week: Radio 1, Radio 2, Radio 3, Radio 4, Radio Luxembourg . . .? (To this list may be added the name of local BBC or commercial stations, and if applicable Radio Scotland or Radio Wales.)
 b At what times of the day do you normally listen to each station?
 c Which type of radio programme would you like to hear more of?
 d Which types of radio programme would you like to hear less of?
 It is also interesting to ascertain some information about the person answering the questions. Professional analysts would want to fit the person into the following categories:
 a Male/Female

b Age: under 15; 15–24; 25–34, 35–54; over 55

c Social class: ABC1 or C2DE

The matter of social class is clearly the most complex, and will need to be treated carefully. The help of a social scientist is essential if the answers are to be valid and if good use is to be made of them.

Records

The chart used by the BBC is the British Market Research Bureau's chart, details of which can be gained from BMRB, 53 The Mall, London W5. Again pupils can check to see if their local area corresponds to the national chart, and a profile of the record-buying habits of the locality can be obtained through the following questions:

a What were the last three LPs you bought?

b What were the last three singles you bought?

c Name any three pieces of music/artists/records that you have enjoyed listening to recently.

These answers can be used to build up a picture of the type of music that people listen to, rather than what record is the most popular, and again if details of age, sex and class are recorded a more detailed analysis can be achieved.

Concerts

Various pieces of research have been undertaken about which concerts people like to go to, the social class of those attending, and so on. Although research of this type is rarely available to the public, schools can contact The Arts Council (105 Piccadilly, London W1) for information on what surveys are currently available. Once again, comparison can then be made with findings obtained by pupils working locally.

With all three surveys put together the school should gain a powerful insight into the musical attitudes and interests of the locality. Pupils can then be asked for their views on the findings, and this can stimulate lively discussion. If, for example, the research confirms that under three per cent of the population go to concerts or listen to Radio 3, can the expenditure of public funds through the Arts Council be justified in this field?

Related resources

School textbooks

T. Attwood and P. Farmer: *Pop Workbook* Edward Arnold, 1978

P. Farmer and T. Attwood: *The Pop Business* Edward Arnold, 1979

T. Attwood: *In Concert* Syston, 1979

T. Attwood: *The Pop Songbook* (2 volumes) OUP, 1981

P. Farmer: *Pop, The Story of Pop, Ragtime and Blues* and *Steelbands and Reggae* (Longman Music Topics Series) Longman

M. Burnett: *Pop Music* (Oxford Topics in Music) OUP, 1980

Other books

Music Week Yearbook: 40 Long Acre, London WC2

Kemps Music and Recording Industry Yearbook: 1–5 Bath St., London EC1

M. Cable: *The Pop Industry Inside Out* W. H. Allen, 1977

G. Vulliamy and E. Lee (eds): *Pop Music in School* CUP, 1976 (2nd edition, 1980)

G. Vulliamy and E. Lee (eds): *Pop, Rock and Ethnic Music in School* CUP, 1981

Trade publications

Music Master: 1 De Cham Ave., Hastings, Sussex
Yearly music catalogue with monthly updates
Music Week: 40 Long Acre, London WC2
Trade magazine
Record Business: Hyde House, 13 Langley St., London WC2
Trade weekly

Popular music papers

Melody Maker: Surrey House, 1 Throwley Way, Sutton, Surrey
Musicians Only: 143 Charing Cross Rd., London WC2
New Musical Express: Kings Reach Tower, Stamford St., London SE1
New Music News: 1/3 Mortimer St., London W1
Record Mirror and *Sounds*: 40 Long Acre, London WC2

© Tony Attwood

Water music

Phil Ellis

Water Music *is the title of a course which was run by Phil Ellis at Notley High School, Braintree, Essex. Although it contains many ideas which could be successful on their own, it is the only chapter in this book which describes a whole course based on a single theme.*

The emphasis of classroom work at Notley was always on practical activity of a flexible and individual nature:

'Pupils were encouraged to make their own musical/artistic statements in their own way rather than imitate/reiterate those of other people.'

To this end departmental money was spent on buying instruments and electronic equipment which would be available for all pupils to use.

The essence of this practical course was the belief in people as they are rather than as others think they ought to be. An attempt was always made to allow for expressive activity to take place constructively, and so a fairly tight structure was provided for younger pupils, within which there was room for a good deal of experimentation:

'As far as possible right/wrong situations were avoided, and great care was taken not to provide "models" at which to aim. The approval of the "teacher" was not held to be important, whereas extending exploratory and expressive work in a variety of media was.'

Water Music, *as described in this chapter, reflects Phil Ellis' personal philosophy of music education, and as a project will appeal not only to those teachers who share this view of school music, but also to those who are simply looking for new and exciting classroom ideas.*

Starting the project

Key Lesson

The first lesson outlined the scope of the course and allowed various worksheets to be distributed. Often several worksheets were stapled together and given to each pupil, including stimulus material and instructions for individual research which was to be undertaken during the term. The feedback from this into practical sessions was obviously very important.

During this first Key Lesson a careful explanation of the homework worksheet would be given. Pupils would be required to work on at least one aspect from A and B, though many would do much more than the stated minimum.

Water Music Worksheet

Choose at least one subject from section A and B, and find out as much as you can about it for homework:

A. Myths and Legends
   Neptune – Greek and Roman water gods and myths
   The Little Mermaid
   The Lorelei Legend
   Marie Celeste
   Jonah and the Whale – Noah – biblical water stories
   Mother Shipton at Knaresborough – petrifying wells
   Loch Ness and other monsters

B. Nature and Science
   Trace the water cycle from a spring – river – sea, and back to spring
   How do tides change?
   Waterfalls, rapids, currents . . . How and where do these occur?
   Underground water. Caves, potholes, wells, stalactites . . .
   Find out about these.
   The sea. Lakes. Ponds. Reflections

Homework generated from this worksheet would continue throughout the term, and often connections occurred between the area being investigated in written work and the practical work being undertaken. It is a good idea to have a large selection of books available which are relevant to the topic. In my own case the local library was very helpful, providing a large box full of useful material for the whole term which supplemented the resources of the school library.

Having covered the aspects of the course which concern research and written work the rest of the first Key Lesson would be spent discussing the practical work to be undertaken. The first piece on any course was usually small in concept, and a time limit would be imposed on it of perhaps two or three weeks. Groups would work on a piece for a length of time and then one lesson would be spent in performances of the completed pieces, each group in turn performing to the rest of the class (this being an important stage in the process) allowing for criticism and suggestion.

First piece

For the first piece fairly severe limitations were imposed in order to focus pupils' attention. Perhaps only two possible choices would be given during the Key Lesson, these taking the following form:

1 Using voices and a tape recorder, construct a piece which imitates:
   a   A dripping tap
   b   Pouring water into a bowl
   c   A flushing lavatory
   d   Water emptying from a bath/sink/drain – noisily
   e   Any combination of these or other water sounds

For this particular piece a portable tape recorder can be invaluable, as recordings of the actual sounds can be made and then listened to closely. Following this, vocal imitations are the first step, with some attempt at notation in the form of graphic representation, or even in the form of poetry, for example, Karl Schwitters' or Edwin Morgan's. Following this a 'score' can be produced so that a repeatable performance can be practised and developed.

Time permitting, resourceful groups may prepare an ordered series of recorded water sounds which can be played back as part of the piece, the vocal element complementing and contrasting with this. Thus from a simple beginning complex decisions have to be made in order for a two- or three-minute piece to be successful. Questions of contrast, colour, shape, dynamic, tempo, texture, etc., can be explored and evaluated both with the individual groups, and later with the whole class when performances are mounted.

2 Using only two types of instrument (e.g. keyboard, pitched percussion, metal percussion, drums, etc. . . .), construct a piece called *The Storm*, and represent this with a score.

Two poetry worksheets

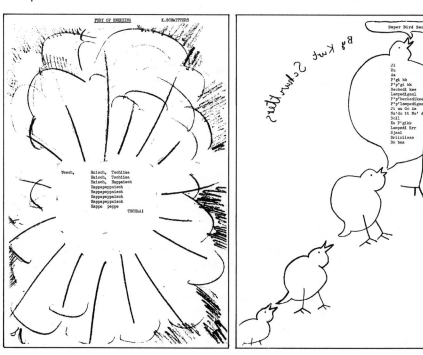

These instructions give a structure for groups to use, and also draw on the personal experience of individuals. Discussion with groups about storms they have experienced is always fruitful and plans for such pieces can usually be seen in four sections:

a   The calm before the storm – all activity gradually ceases – a sense of foreboding – tension – gathering darkness.

b   The first raindrops which gradually increase in frequency – distant thunder coming closer – coldness – driving wind.

c   The climax of the storm and the piece – lightning, thunder, hailstones, wind – followed by a gradual calming.

d   The aftermath (coda!) – storm clouds slowly disappear – sun returns – warmer – brighter – clean – fresh – bird song.

There are obvious sound parallels here, but there is also an emotional aspect to consider: the change from peace to a sense of foreboding, tension, fear, violence, conflict, and then resolution, a different feeling of peace, being clean, refreshed, new. This emotional 'programme' is important and much fruitful discussion, activity and expression can develop from it.

More advanced work

Groups will be given several worksheets in addition to the homework worksheet already discussed, and these contain suggestions for further work of a more extended nature. Having completed the first assignment, where little real choice was possible, groups at this stage may enjoy considerably more freedom. Some groups may care to choose a worksheet and not depart from the instructions at all; other groups may take an idea from a worksheet and develop it in their own way. Groups often devise extended projects lasting several weeks and involving many different disciplines.

Thus later lessons would present several worksheets consisting of instructions, suggestions, pictures, poems, etc. Groups could use them as they stood, react against them and produce alternative ideas, or completely ignore them, although only rarely did this third possibility occur. Examples are given below.

Ideas developing from art

On a small scale, two of Paul Klee's drawings were useful as starting points. *Play on the water* looks as much like the grain seen in a piece of wood as anything else. However, the suggestions printed below this picture were as follows:

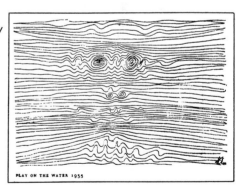

PLAY ON THE WATER 1935

Change
Is this water into face?
Is this face into water?
How many 'things' can you 'see' in the drawing?
What connects them?

Sound the picture
Choose your instruments carefully – you will
have to justify your choice

Static – change – static
Calm – rough – calm
Simple – rough – simple
Safe – dangerous – safe

A second Klee drawing, *Migrating fish*, was given similar treatment, with suggestions for possible developments being made. A more emotive picture was duplicated as another worksheet. One of Doré's illustrations from *Rime of the Ancient Mariner* was used. This depicts a ghost ship (in the eyes of pupils) covered in ice, surrounded by icebergs and complete with an albatross flying above. The caption reads . . .

'. . . it grew wondrous cold: And ice, mast-high,
came drifting by, as green as emerald.'

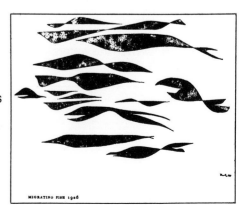

MIGRATING FISH 1926

The suggestions printed beneath this picture read:

Write a poem in free verse or a descriptive passage/story which expresses your feelings about the picture.
Give your writing a title.
Create a piece of music which complements the picture and your writing.
Having completed your music, devise a mime to further express the atmosphere and feelings of the piece.

By suspending a large sheet in front of different coloured lights most evocative shadows can be cast on to the sheet 'screen' lending additional atmosphere to mimes. Similarly, abstract slides can be produced, and if these are projected over a group performance the piece becomes more powerful still. It is important that positive feedback results from performances; not all groups can produce outstanding work, but when a really successful piece results it can produce considerable enthusiasm in a whole class and generate many additional ideas.

Ideas from section A of homework worksheet

A more lengthy, ambitious structure was generated from the story of Noah. A suggested form was duplicated for groups to use should they wish, but often a group would develop their own ideas on this and other stories. This worksheet was in 15 sections.

Noah

1. Music to suggest springtime – peace – a beginning – tranquillity.
2. The above music continuing, but now as background to the following words:
   When man began to multiply on the face of the earth and daughters were born to them, the sons of god saw that the daughters of man were fair. But the Lord saw that the wickedness of man was great on the earth and that his thoughts were evil. The Lord was sorry that he had made man and said: 'I WILL BLOT OUT MAN WHO I CREATED FROM THE FACE OF THE EARTH AND EVERY LIVING CREATURE SHALL DIE FOR I AM SORRY TO HAVE CREATED THEM.'
3. A very brief musical interlude, full of menace and foreboding, but becoming optimistic, leading into and accompanying
4. 'But Noah found favour in the eyes of God and he said to Noah . . .
   "GO AND BUILD YOURSELF AN ARK FOR I AM GOING TO BRING A GREAT FLOOD. TAKE WITH YOU INTO THE ARK YOUR FAMILY AND TWO OF EVERY LIVING CREATURE."
   Noah did all that he was commanded.'
5. Music to represent the building of the ark. This section could suggest the hard work and endless labour with the use of repeating rhythmical patterns.
6. 'When the waters of the flood came, two of every living creature entered the ark.'
7. An enormous procession. The music at first very quiet but becoming extremely loud. A rhythmical, perhaps tuneful, section with some suggestions of the different types of animal represented in the music.
   A sudden silence . . .
8. Music, very sparse at first, to suggest the approach of the rains, storms, floods, deaths . . . This could continue softly through 9.
9. 'The flood continued for forty days upon the earth and even the highest mountains were covered. All living things outside the ark were killed.'
10. Music as at the ending of 8 but developed into a representation of the forty days of rain and storm etc.
11. 'But God remembered Noah and he made the waters subside until the earth was dry.'
12. Music to represent the gradual drying of the earth.
13. 'Then God said to Noah
    "GO FORTH WITH YOUR FAMILY AND THE ANIMALS OUT OF THE ARK FOR I AM ANGRY NO MORE." '
14. Music as in section 7 only this time starting very loud and exciting and gradually fading away into the distance.
15. A suitable coda could be music of 14 fading into a repeat of the opening music to show a new beginning peace, tranquillity, leading to the appearance of the rainbow.

Any group attempting this piece exactly as suggested would obviously need a tape recorder in order to store each section as it was finished, and so gradually build up the complete piece. Several tape techniques can be exploited: loops of rhythmic ostinato can be combined in section 5; sensitive use of recording levels in sections 7 and 14 may seem obvious but can be very telling. As part of the music for section 5, a recording could be made of the woodwork/metalwork rooms and this superimposed with other, less random sounds.

An obvious link with art for a group working this piece is for them to produce a series of drawings or paintings illustrating the story. These can be made into slides so that the finished piece in performance would be a tape/slide sequence combining music, words and art.

Free developments from this section of the worksheet included groups devising dances to complement tapes of their music based on water nymphs. This involved designing and making costumes so that the project became extending in many areas. (An example of this can be seen in the first part of the tape/slide sequence *Music at Notley*, S.C.M.P. University of York, 1977.)

Another source which led to extended composition was taken from *The Dance and the Drum* by Elizabeth and John Paynter (Universal Edition, 1974). 'How the Land of Yoruba was Formed' is a short legend, its brevity contributing to its usefulness. From this story a worksheet can be devised similar to the Noah legend above.

Ideas from section B of homework worksheet

Pieces connected with this section of the worksheet can be structured quite easily. For example, the water cycle could be ordered as follows:

Water vapour
Condensation
Mist
Rain
Water landing on earth
Water seeping through the ground
A spring
A stream
A river
Waterfall
Rapids
The sea
Evaporation
Water vapour

Not all these stages need be included in a piece, but it has a clear cyclic structure and many musical ideas can be generated from the different stages noted above. Various kinds of instrument, texture and technique are fairly obvious (you won't need drums for water vapour!) and thus it provides a group with a large-scale composition which is easily seen in small sections, each requiring careful thought yet leading to the construction of a complex whole.

More lengthy pieces exploiting tape techniques are also possible developments from this section of the worksheet. The first piece (page 63) using voices and water sounds can be extended at this stage. Looping, speed changing, reversal, etc., tend to be time-consuming activities, and groups attempting such work invariably need a lot of help, but the results are often very exciting.

The effect of using a tape recorder to slow sound down was often used. A cymbal slowed down changes into an immense gong, vocal sounds become eerie and mysterious, claves sound like water dripping in an immense cavern, drum beats become heart beats, and so on. Pieces with titles such as *Caves*, *Underground*, *Underwater*, etc., made the exploitation of such techniques particularly apposite.

Cave project

A large-scale piece which can be developed, and which can exploit many different techniques and areas of expression, can be found in the general theme of *underground*. It provides an excellent excuse to organize an outing to caves if

Speedwell Cavern, Castleton, Derbyshire

there are some near. I have used Wookey Hole in Somerset as the basis for a large-scale piece, although any cave system, real or imagined, is appropriate.

Wookey Hole seems to be a good choice as there are several associations which can be very inspiring, in addition to the atmosphere of underground caverns and water sounds, etc. Here is a brief description of Wookey Hole:

The entrance to the caverns is an opening into the side of a hill beneath overhanging rocks. This is the entrance to the Great Cave. A sloping passage leads to Hell's Ladder, a steep flight of steps which descend to the first great chamber known as the Witch's Kitchen. In this chamber it is possible to see the river Axe which flows through the system, and also the stalagmite figure of the Witch of Wookey. It seems that at some period of history this cavern was the scene of mysterious rites, as large numbers of human bones and remains have been excavated in the sandbank above the river. This chamber is immense, the roof being 130 feet high, and many entrances to inaccessible passages are visible.

From this chamber is a steep flight of steps leading to grottoes where various stalactites and stalagmites of differing colours can be seen. The second chamber is known as the Hall of Wookey, and here is also the island of stalagmite known as St Michael's Mount. This hall abounds with stalactites, the roof being 80 feet high. The third chamber is known as the Witch's Parlour and is nowhere higher than ten feet, although it is 135 feet in diameter. Many eerie sounds can often be heard in these caverns and early man connected them with the wrath of the gods of the underworld.

The legend of the Witch of Wookey can be discussed and embroidered. (Some of the evidence of cannibalism from the nearby Hyena's Den also provides some inspiration for a few!) Such a description could be accompanied by slides, and so presented in as atmospheric a way as possible. (Speaking through a reverberation unit at appropriate moments is quite effective!) It could provide enough stimulus for one term. In addition to the tape techniques mentioned earlier which are evocative of subterranean sounds, an extended music/theatre event can be constructed combining as many different media as possible. For example:

1. **Introduction** Music suggesting sunlight, warmth, happiness.
2. **Entrance** Change from light to dark, from warmth to cold, happiness to unease.
3. **Great Cave** Scope here for an evocative piece exploiting echoes, reverberation and slowed-down sound.
4. **Descent** Hell's Ladder – the title alone is usually sufficient to suggest all sorts of ideas – music with slides.
5. **Witch's Kitchen** Excellent opportunity for some theatre or mime at this stage, plus the use of words (poetry?) for the witch. A climax of excitement in the acting out of sacrificial rites, combining theatre and music. Costumes and props can be built, and slides projected during this section can be particularly effective.
6. **Hall of Wookey** Less dramatic – more abstract. Use of organs, cymbals, voices, all slowed down and echoed to represent the grandeur of the chamber.
7. **Witch's Parlour** The darkest, most claustrophobic section. (Some may care to produce a piece based on claustrophobia to be included here.) The eerie sounds of the angry gods of the underworld are an additional possibility.
8. **Coda** A brief reference to the preceding sections, but in reverse order, as we return to the surface. The change from darkness and unreality to light and the safety of day.

This 'trip' can provide endless scope for extended composition and expression, in which poetry, theatre, art work, slide projection, making of props and costumes, dance, mime and lighting effects can all be combined and exploited.

Related activities

Included in *Water Music* was a poem sheet. Often worksheets specified that poems should be written and collected on the subject. A two-sided poem sheet was prepared, reflecting the many different styles and viewpoints of various poets. Such poems were used in a variety of ways: as a structure, as mood settings, as words for songs, as words to be read, intoned or chanted whilst music is played. Often such poetry would be augmented by verses written by people in one of the groups.

An additional aspect of this course involved the use of water as a medium for distorting sound or generating effects particularly in conjunction with simple electronics. From a purely acoustic point of view, metal instruments make very beautiful glissandos when lowered into water (or raised out of it). Cymbals and tubular bells are particularly effective when used in this way. Controlling the rate at which air escapes from an inflated balloon by holding and stretching the neck under water can also yield very interesting and controllable aural events, as can the use of pipes to feed vocal sounds through water.

We acquired a large tank from a domestic water system which was being replaced because it leaked. The metalwork department sealed the leaks and so we obtained a large, watertight metal tank at no cost. (Old washing machine tubs and baths can be very useful.) In addition to the effects already noted, recording underwater proved to be interesting. Some cheap contact microphones were bought. These were already encased in rubber and we tried to make them waterproof by coating the joints with rubber solution. By attaching these to the sides of the tank, or on to instruments which were then lowered into the water, or merely suspending them in the tank at various depths and locations, a variety of interesting sounds could be recorded. It was a fascinating experiment, and considerable interest was aroused from a technical as well as aural point of view. Further developments included the attempt to make a loudspeaker waterproof so that virtually any sound could be played underwater at high volume.

A small fish tank was available in the art department. This was filled with water, and then small amounts of oil-based coloured inks were dropped on to the surface of the water. A sheet of paper was carefully laid on the water and then removed. Beautiful flowing abstract patterns were produced in this way as some of the ink was transferred to the paper. When dry these could be used as 'scores' for musical purposes, different colours representing different instruments, intensity representing volume or speed.

Numerous slides were available for use. These were of various water scenes: the sea in various moods, waterfalls, rapids, lakes, ponds, rivers, and rain. Having a slide, or sequence of slides to work from is a great aid, focusing the attention, inspiring the imagination and providing atmosphere. Often these would be most effective when combined with poetry or drama.

Throughout the course there are moments when recorded music relevant to the theme could be played to classes. At appropriate moments individual groups can be usefully directed towards specific pieces of music which complement their work, but always after they have completed a piece. Thus a group who have attempted some work on water sounds and tape techniques may find Takemitsu's *Water Music* of interest. Much of Debussy's piano music is also relevant, especially if a group has produced music using keyboards, glockenspiels or xylophones. Other suitable music includes Debussy's *La Mer* and Britten's *Four Sea Interludes*.

Related bibliography

P. Klee: *On Modern Art* Faber and Faber, 1966
A short treatise on modern art containing many examples of Klee's drawings and insights into the processes of composition which are readily connected with music.

Schools Council: *Music at Notley* Schools Council York Music Project, 1977
A 30-minute tape/slide sequence which describes aspects of curriculum music which I developed whilst at Notley High School. Several courses, similar to *Water Music*, are discussed and illustrated.

E. and J. Paynter: *The Dance and the Drum* Universal Edition
A book containing 12 projects, all based on myths and legends. Ideas are given on encouraging music-theatre as a classroom activity.

T. Wishart: *Sun* Universal Edition
A description of several projects which were put into practice prior to the writing of the book: a creative approach to the world around us, not limited to the classroom or any single aspect of 'education'.

© Phil Ellis

Music and integrated arts studies

Joan Arnold

In just over ten years of organized existence, integrated studies has already gone through the predictable pendulum-like phases of all new educational ideas. In the early 1970s 'I.S.' or 'I.D.E.' was widespread, though mainly for humanities-based subjects, and was institutionalized by the Schools Council Keele Project (1968–72) as well as numerous scale posts in secondary schools.

But regrettably, as with so many of the so-called progressive ideas of the 1960s and early 1970s, 'public opinion' as well as teacher opinion has turned against those who pioneered integrated work. There are now many schools which have reverted to single subject teaching where previously subjects had been grouped together under the umbrella of a 'faculty' or 'subject co-ordinator'.

Ironically, the quiet progress made by aesthetic subjects in integration has been rather more steady than that of the humanities, perhaps because these subjects receive less attention from the public. This has resulted in a good deal of successful integration in schools, including Frogmore School, Camberley, where Joan Arnold is in charge of Creative Arts.

In writing this chapter Joan Arnold has put together a programme of musical work and related activities based on topics which she has found successful in her own teaching. The three programmes are particularly geared to specific age groups and one (Christmas project) is planned for a particular time of year. Each programme is designed to last about six weeks (half a term) and is intended to show how practical work around a theme can be developed to form a logical unit of work, progressing from simple to more complicated ideas.

While Joan Arnold would not in any way suggest that one should tackle other areas of creative work, either within the music lesson or parallel to it, she is saying that one can. She has certainly found that the work produced in music in her school has been of a higher standard when stimulated by a variety of creative activity.

PROGRAMME 1

Animals

(1st year secondary level)

Practical work	Related musical work	Related creative activities
Movement pieces	Rhythms & word patterns	Drama: The Hunter & the
Sound pieces	Singing/playing songs	Hunted (game), Acting out animal story
Animal songs	Listening: Carnival of the	Dance, Animal movements
Animal stories	Animals, Peter and the Wolf	Art/Pottery: drawings, paintings
Noah	Noye's Fludde, Captain Noah,	wall frieze, masks, costumes,
Taping animal sounds	First Cuckoo (Delius)	back cloth, animal tiles

WEEK 1

I have timed the Animal project to follow a visit to the zoo, but this cannot always be arranged. Starting a project on animals, it is useful to take a particular discussion point. It could be any one of the following: domestic animals, wild animals, hunting instincts, the cat family, man and hunting, the retriever dog, the tracker dog, hounds, voice pitches, camouflage and movement. There are many others which you may like to choose.

Looking at pictures, slides and films of animals always helps discussion as does an attractive wall display. I try to finish the discussions with animal movement because it leads nicely into the first piece of practical work.

Practical work 1

Divide the class into groups of 4–6. Ask them to choose a speed and style of movement, for example slow and crawling like a snail or fast and hopping like a kangaroo. Using word sounds only, ask them to make up a piece to describe the animal. Make them say the words the way they want the animal to sound. They can choose words that describe the particular animal, for example for the snail, 'slow', 'slimy', 'slithery', etc. Give them time and then get each group to perform its piece. If they keep the identity of their animal a secret, the others in the class can try to guess it.

Related activities

Drama or movement work can be done on the way animals move. This can be done as mime or as dance to music; Saint-Saëns's *Carnival of the Animals* is a good piece to use. Drawings or paintings of the chosen animals can be made and relief tiles of the animals' heads can be modelled.

WEEK 2

In the second week I concentrate on animal sounds. In class discussion I would encourage pupils to pick out sounds which are typical of particular animals or types of animals, for example horses' hooves, the call of a cuckoo, the croak of a frog, the hissing of a snake and the squeaking of a mouse. It is quite a good idea to give the class five minutes to write down as many animal sounds as possible. This gives them plenty to contribute to the discussion.

Practical work 2

Keeping the same small groups as before, give each group one animal to work with. With instruments and voices they have to make up a piece which is based on the sound that the animal makes. A cuckoo piece for example, could be based on the interval of a major third, a horse's piece on the brisk 2/4 rhythm of four trotting quavers (plus coconut shells!) These musical ideas (major third and 2/4 quavers) would have to be explained first. Here are two examples:

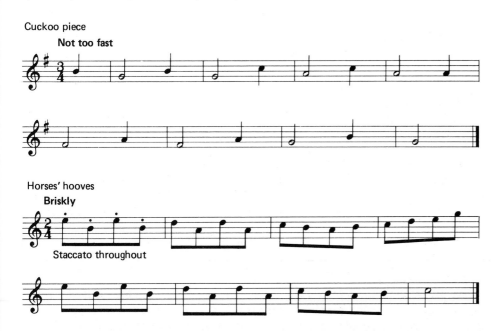

Cuckoo piece
Not too fast

Horses' hooves
Briskly

Staccato throughout

It is necessary to choose instruments very carefully. The horses' hooves sound better on a wooden xylophone with hard beaters than on a metallophone or glockenspiel, but the cuckoo piece might sound better on a metal instrument. The children should be encouraged to think for themselves and to be critical of the sounds they make. Don't let them forget their own voices; the best snake hiss is probably made with the voice. Don't forget to allow time for a play through.

Related activities

A frieze of animals could be put together and pinned on the wall. Drawings and paintings done in the first week could contribute to this and some sort of background painted in.

In drama, the game *The Hunter and the Hunted* is always popular, and it makes the class concentrate and listen for sounds. Sit the class in a large circle.

One child, the hunter, is blindfolded and stands in the middle of the circle. Another child is the hunted and has no blindfold but must remain on hands and knees. The idea is for the hunted to move around as quietly as he can and to avoid being caught by the hunter. The hunter must listen carefully for sounds of movement and must try to catch his prey. Occasionally the hunted can make animal sounds to attract the hunter's attention.

WEEK 3

As a preliminary to practical work 3, I use the Flanders and Swann animal songs. The children enjoy listening to them and joining in. There are parts of the piano accompaniment which are very descriptive, and one can make a useful listening exercise out of this.

At this stage ask the pupils to make up an animal poem of their own. It can be humorous; it need not rhyme but *it must have a good rhythm*. Here, work on simple word patterns needs to be done to help them organize their poems. This might also be an ideal opportunity to involve a colleague in the English department, for the poems could be written in an English lesson.

Practical work 3

Once in their working groups, get the children to choose the best poem in their group, and ask them to make up a tune to go with the words, stressing the rhythm work done beforehand. Movement and sound ideas used in weeks 1 and 2 may be used again and it is often a good idea to limit their choice of notes, perhaps to a pentatonic scale. Usually the most difficult thing is to get the right *metre* and I spend a lot of time with each group making sure they understand this.

Related activities

Work can be continued on the frieze, and if the pottery tile has been biscuit fired the glazing can be done. It may also be possible to choose an animal song to make into a dance, for example *The Gnu song* or *The Hippopotamus song*. Both these have a story element and would be effective as mime or movement.

WEEKS 4 AND 5

The next practical work is the making of a musical story rather like *Peter and the Wolf* by Prokofiev, so we spend some time listening to it. It includes a number of the things the children have already done, for example, descriptions of the sounds the animals make, like the bird's song, the duck's quack and the wolf's growl. It is a good idea to give the children things to listen for, for example, 'Which instrument plays the bird?', and 'Why do you think Prokofiev chose it?' In addition, the idea of a *motif* or *theme* for each character must be explained.

Practical work 4

Following on from the Prokofiev, ask each group to make up their own animal story. This will have to be written down carefully as it will be *narrated*; the idea of a narrator must also be clarified. Next, each group must list the animals and people involved and make a tune or theme for each of them. This can take some time, so some of the earlier practical pieces may be used. The story can then be performed with narration and music.

Related activities

In drama, these stories may be acted out and masks may be made. These can be very simple. Cut the basic face from a piece of coloured sugar paper. Tie on string or tape to fasten at the back. Cut out eyes, nose (if necessary) and mouth and add tissue paper, string for fur, whiskers, etc. This can be done with white card, which is stronger and can be made three-dimensional quite easily.

Masks are most effective if worn with black costumes (black trousers, sweaters and socks or black leotards).

1 Rectangular Card

2 Cut out oval shape

face size

3 Cut for folding

4 Fold over side pieces and stick onto centre piece so making it three-dimensional

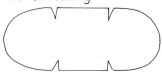

5

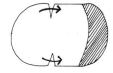

Add ears, whiskers etc. Cut out eyes. Fix ties

WEEKS 6 AND 7
There are a number of musical works based on the story of Noah and so it
seems quite a good idea to end the animal project with a classroom version. I
have used *Captain Noah's Floating Zoo* as singing material and have used parts
of Britten's *Noye's Fludde* as listening material. I have also found the procession
of animals going two by two most useful as a stimulus for practical work.

Practical work 5

This is a class version of Noah. First the whole class work on the actual story
line. When this is completed give each group part of the story on which to work.
You must decide whether the whole thing is going to be sung or whether there is
to be a narrator (this is easier). All the animal songs, tunes and sounds done
before may be used and some new material composed. Some simple divisions
could be:
1. God's warning.
2. The building of the Ark.
3. The rain starts.
4. The animals' procession.
5. The flood.
6. Homecoming.

Related activities
If this is to be performed, costumes and scenery have to be made. Movement
sequences should be devised and parts rehearsed and learned.
    These two last projects may well take longer than the time suggested. It might
be that it is better to concentrate on one of them only, for four weeks. If this is a
team teaching situation, the production could well be the end product of the
various units of work.

PROGRAMME 2

Christmas

(2nd year secondary level)

Practical work	Related musical work	Related creative activities
Carols (words and music) Themes for characters Arrangements Christmas story	Carol singing Verse/chorus/rondo form Character themes – leitmotiv Listening: Amahl & the Night Visitors, Xmas Jazz, Carols.	Acting out Xmas story Customs & traditions/Mummers Wassailing Xmas in Australia Movement: the Carole, a round dance Frieze Carol book cover Christmas card Stained glass window Puppets Costumes Crib scene

WEEK 1
It is easy to assume that all children know the Christmas story, but I always start
this project with a brief resumé just in case! In this first session I also discuss the
various things that we do for Christmas. It is amazing for example, how different
our Christmas day routines are. Some families open all their presents all together
before breakfast, some wait until the evening and so on.

Practical work 1a

This is making up Christmas carols. I sometimes make this into a competition with winning entries performed at a Christmas music evening. It is a good idea to list possible themes: The Star, The Three Kings, The Shepherds, Searching for a room, The Lullaby, etc. It is also useful to sing through a few well-known carols and discuss them. Next divide the class into groups and ask each group to make up words for their carol. Remind them about rhyme and rhythm. (If the Animal project has been tackled in the first year this will not be new to them.) If a carol is to be successful it must have a catchy tune and often repeated lines of melody help this.

Get them to make up tunes for their words. Discuss ideas like **verse** and **chorus** and perhaps **rondo form**. Consider also their own vocal range; remind them that they must be able to sing their own carol and therefore the tune must flow.

Related activities

Art work could include the designing of a cover for a carol book. (I sometimes collect together all the carols written in one project and make them into a book.) A frieze of the Christmas story could be made for the music room. I show slides of Jerusalem and Bethlehem but any relevant visual material you can find will stimulate them.

WEEK 2

It is very probable that the first practical work (1a) will not be completed and I therefore use the second week to do this. Some of the faster working groups will be finished and ready to tackle something new; others will still be struggling to finish the words. (For these pupils omit practical work 1b.)

Practical work 1b

Now ask each group to make another arrangement of their carol, using classroom percussion instruments and any orchestral instruments that they are able to play. Different accompanying rhythms may be used, for example Latin-american rhythms, or Spanish ones like this *Habanera* rhythm:

Instruments like maracas, tambourine and drums can be used effectively, as can the guitar. I usually ask pupils to stress the vocal line so that the idea of a Christmas *song* is retained.

Related activities

The **Carole** was originally a round dance. A group might like to make up the steps for a round dance to a well-known carol tune. Others might like to find out about old Christmas customs like the wassailing bowl, mummers and mystery plays.

WEEK 3

Practical work 2a

Following on from the work done on arranging the original carols, arranging well-known carols is a very useful activity. The completed arrangements can be used in Christmas concerts and the whole class can join in the performance. I usually do an arrangement myself first, so that the pupils understand what they have to do. A simple three-part arrangement with a strong rhythmic percussion part is usually successful. Here is an example that you can try out. Divide the class into four groups giving one part to each group to learn.

As you can see, the first two parts are slightly more complicated than the third part, which I have kept as simple as possible (four notes) so that the less able children will be able to play it. The minim-crotchet rhythm will give them something to work at.

Any instrumentalists you have in the class could be asked to make up a descant of their own to improvise over the top. The rhythm percussion part is to be played gently to give the idea of a rocking rhythm; perhaps the drums could be played with the hands.

Practical work 2b

Now ask the class to make their own arrangement of a well-known carol. I usually choose one with them and ask each group to learn to play it and to provide one counter-melody and one accompanying rhythm. This way, if you are lucky, when you put them all together they should fit (with a little adaptation!). Some good carols to try are: *Good King Wenceslas, In Dulce Jubilo, O Come all ye Faithful* and *Silent Night.* Be careful to choose an easy key and one that is within the range of all the instruments you are using.

Related activities

Christmas is an ideal time for the model-maker. Get the class to make a crib scene. This could be made from a variety of materials. Each child could be responsible for an animal or character and the whole thing could be done in clay.

Joan Arnold

At this stage, the pupils have quite a good repertoire of Christmas music. They can play their own carols, or arrangements of well-known ones, and they have sung through quite a number all together. Now I find it satisfying to draw all this work together into some sort of story. To do this we need music for the main characters.

Practical work 3a

With the whole class, decide on the main characters; for example Joseph, Mary, Baby Jesus, Three Kings, Shepherds, etc. Separate into working groups and give each group one character on which to work. The theme music can take the form of a song or simply some descriptive music, but it must be easily recognizable and simple to play.

Some helpful ideas may be given; for example, the use of the pentatonic scale for the three kings from the orient and lullaby music for the baby Jesus.

Related activities

I have found that rather than acting out the story ourselves, it has been great fun to make a puppet version. Each group could make the character for which they have composed music. A puppet theatre must also be built. This can be done quite simply with cardboard boxes, but it must be firm and large enough to hide the puppeteers. Shadow puppets may be used as an alternative. This is an ideal project in which to involve drama and art colleagues.

WEEK 6
This is the week for putting everything together and rehearsing it for a performance. Any pupils who feel that puppets are too 'childish' for them are usually quite happy to perform for *other* children, such as the local primary school.

Practical work 3b

Play through the whole Christmas story. Check the order first and insert any narration or dialogue that is necessary. If you are going to perform it as a puppet play, make sure your puppeteers are not needed to play the music. This may mean swapping parts. Alternatively, tape all the music first. Timing is important; make sure that each piece of music is the right length for the action it plays for. This might mean repeating some parts and cutting others.

Related activities

All the puppets should be completed, but if not now is the time to finish them. As it will be nearing Christmas, it is a good time to be making cards and labels, lanterns and stained-glass windows.

For the last, you will need some black sugar paper, coloured tissue paper, scissors and glue. First design a picture for your window. Draw it out in rough with double outlines. Next, draw it out on to the sugar paper and cut out the spaces. Remember not to cut the outlines away from the frame. Finally, cut out shapes in coloured tissue paper and stick them on to the back of the window.

These are most effective stuck on to windows, so that the light shines through.

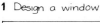
1 Design a window

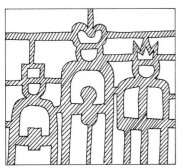
2 Draw it out with a double outline

3 Stick coloured tissue paper to the back.

PROGRAMME 3

Variations

(3rd year secondary level)

Practical work	Related musical work	Related creative activities
Variation on well-known tune. 8–12 bar original theme & variations Ground bass (small group and class group)	Change in music/time/speed/dynamics/mood/mode/major/minor/harmonies/counter melodies/descants *Listening* Mahler: Symphony No. 1 Saint-Saëns: Carnival (tortoise) Pachelbel: Kanon Ravel: Bolero Elgar: Enigma Variations Lloyd Webber: Variations	Drama: change in social values Victorian standards Dance: characters from Enigma Art: lettering, change of fashions, design for a record sleeve

WEEK 1

'What is another word meaning to *change*?' This is the question with which I usually start this project. Eventually we end up with to *vary* and *variation*. Next I ask the class to write down all the different ways they can think of to change a piece of music. Ideas like slower, faster, adding notes, taking notes away, major/minor, different keys, all emerge. I play one or two examples, taking a well-known tune like the National Anthem, and play it in several different ways.

Before embarking on the practical work I play through the slow movement from Mahler's First Symphony. The Funeral of a French Huntsman uses the 'Frère Jacques' theme most effectively and is a good introduction to variation form. Get the class to write down how they think the music changes.

Practical work 1a

This is to play several versions of 'Frère Jacques'; first play the original theme (changed to accommodate the range of classroom instruments) and then changed versions. I usually put these on an overhead projector sheet so they can all see, and we play them together.

Practical work 1b

Each small group has the task of adding one more variation of 'Frère Jacques' to the Variation Bank, so that by the end of the first week we may have as many as fifteen variations.

Related activities

Write down the word Variation in as many different ways as possible (types of lettering, size, etc.). Also, use a dictionary of synonyms to find as many variations of the word variation as you can!

WEEK 2

After the first week's experience of playing different versions of the same tune it is a good idea to listen to one or two more sets of variations. Ravel's *Bolero* is a good example of the same tune played by different instruments, with a steady increase in dynamics and orchestral texture. 'The Tortoise' from Saint-Saëns's *Carnival of the Animals* is also a good example showing how different a tune can sound if it is slowed down drastically. (See if the children can recognize the tune of the 'can-can'.)

Practical work 2

Ask each group to choose a well-known tune, to play it and to make up three variations. Some good tunes to use are: the National Anthem, *O When the Saints go Marching in, Greensleeves, Three Blind Mice* and *Baa Baa Black Sheep*. Some pupils will spend a long time just learning to play their tunes; encourage them to choose easy ones. Other groups may manage more than just three variations. Leave time to hear a contribution from each group.

Related activities

Fashions have changed considerably over the last 80 years. Ask pupils to trace back styles of clothing to those their great-grandparents wore. Some pupils might be interested in doing the same thing for cars and buses.

WEEK 3

Elgar's *Enigma Variations* is not an easy piece to listen to, but I have found it much easier to approach using *Portraits in Music 1* by David Jenkins and Mark Visocchi (see Resources, page 95). There are excellent illustrations and musical examples which make it easy to follow the shape of the original theme and how it changes in the variations. I do not use all the variations, just the ones that describe the more colourful characters and have the most obvious changes in them. The children seem to like to hear C.A.E. (Elgar's wife) and R.B.T. (Richard Baxter Townshend); these show clearly a rhythmic change and a change from minor to major. Troyte is an exciting variation using the rhythm of the first phrase and Nimrod, the impressive slow variation, is a must. I like to play G.R.S. (George Robertson Sinclair) because of the allusion to his bulldog Dan – this appeals to the children. I rarely play any complete variation; the extracts would be too long for the children's level of concentration.

Practical work 3a

This week I ask the class to make their own theme and variations. This usually takes a long time, and so I suggest that you run it over two or three weeks. During the first week, a simple 8–12 bar theme should be composed. Suggest that it begins and ends on the same (key) note and that a simple rhythm is used. At this stage, I often suggest a 'halfway-house' note. Note 1 is the key note and after four bars you should be at the halfway-house note. The tune should have returned to the key note at the end. If the groups have a fluent main theme at the end of this session then they are well on their way.

Related activities

Make up a dance that illustrates change in direction. Having done that, make up a dance for each of Elgar's Enigma characters. There is in fact a ballet called *Enigma Variations*, which is danced to Elgar's music.

WEEK 4

Practical work 3b

Having written their themes, each group should now be ready to make up their variations. If they need help, get them to try to think of people they know to put into their variations, just as Elgar did with his (for example, if someone is good at sport, they might write a fast variation and the lazy person would deserve a slow-moving variation).

WEEK 5

Pachelbel's *Kanon* and 'Dido's Lament' from Purcell's *Dido and Aeneas* are excellent examples of the ground bass. This form is a good way of leading into work on harmony, but need not be a complicated exercise. Listen to them with the class; see how many times the ground basses appear. At the very end of Brahms's *Variations on a theme of Haydn*, the St Anthony Variations, there is a small phrase in the minor which recurs like a ground bass. It is another good example.

Practical work 4a

Once the group has grasped the idea of a ground bass, give pupils a simple one on which to work. It could be a twelve-bar blues sequence or just one you've made up, for example:

   This particular line used the pentatonic scale. Write it in the bass clef; I use the bass clef as often as I can at this stage, otherwise pupils never learn it. Ask each group to make up three variations to go on top of that bass, stressing that of course the time in this set of variations must remain the same.

Related activities

Having made their variations ask them to design a record sleeve cover for them. Have a good look at some, particularly the one for the Lloyd Webber *Variations*.

WEEK 6

Practical work 4b

Having made their variations to go against the ground bass, the groups should be ready to play them through. Pupils can play the bass line until it is their turn to play above the bass, and all the different group efforts should combine to make one long piece – if you're lucky!

Related resources

Bibliography

J. Arnold: *The Organization of small group work in the classroom.* Schools Council Working Paper 5 from Schools Council Project: Music in the Secondary School curriculum.

D. Jenkins and M. Visocchi: *Portraits in Music 1* OUP, 1980
   Collection of pieces for listening with notes, pictures and ideas for follow-up work. (See also *Portraits in Music 2*.)

H. Chappell: *Xmas Jazz* Clarabella Music Ltd.
   The Bethlehem story as seen through the eyes of the animals and the shepherds.

M. Callaghan and G. Williams: *Shapes and Structures in Music* OUP, 1983
An introduction to musical form based on a workbook and cassette of examples.

Discography

Carnival of the Animals Saint-Saëns   CFP 40086
Peter and the Wolf Prokofiev   CFP 185
Noye's Fludde Britten   ZK1
Captain Noah Horovitz   ZDA 149
On hearing the First Cuckoo in Spring Delius   CFP 40304
At the Drop of a Hat Flanders & Swann   PCS 3001
The Bestiary Flanders & Swann   PCS 3026
Amahl and the Night Visitors Menotti   LSB 4075
Symphony No. 1 Mahler   CFP 40264
Kanon Pachelbel   SDD 411
Bolero Ravel   CFP 40036
Enigma Variations Elgar   CBS 76529
Variations Lloyd Webber   MCF 2824
Rhapsody on a Theme of Paganini Rachmaninov   CFP 40267
Variations on a Nursery Theme Dohnányi   Turnabout TV 34623

Ideas for rhythm

Brian Dennis

Brian Dennis

Many of the 'creative' ideas which have evolved over the past 20 years have provided a highly imaginative and often 'instant' approach to class music-making. Some teachers have used these techniques sparingly while others have applied them with great vigour. Brian Dennis has, however, found that even among the latter a point is often reached (sometimes after several years of creative work) where it is difficult to progress any further:

> *'Ideas seem to bend back on themselves. It is at this point that musical techniques which may well have been taught in more traditional ways (or even through the pop approach) alongside the 'free' approach, could well be brought into play. In other words one should at this stage encourage a 'creative' method, which either helps to develop or at least makes use of traditional skills, albeit in an imaginative way. The class improvisations, compositions and other activities which are so much the hallmark of the creative approach can then acquire a new dimension.'*

It is precisely this background which has encouraged the development of the rhythmic work and ideas contained in this chapter. The material has been designed to satisfy teachers who prefer to avoid dealing constantly with conventional notation (though the ideas can lead to notation if required) as well as those who regard the acquisition of a strong sense of rhythm and beat as something useful in itself.

The two projects which follow are 'Jungle telegraph', a way of transmitting simple rhythmic messages by code, and 'Rhythm squares', which Brian Dennis first used as far back as 1964 but which he has extended here for the purposes of this chapter. Each, used sparingly (neither is intended to be anything like a full course in rhythm) should prove both novel and enjoyable for pupils, while helping them to develop skills in this important area of music education.

PROJECT 1

Jungle telegraph

This consists of developing direct or indirect codes which can be used between pairs or groups of pupils in class. The easiest way to start is first to establish a very simple code which can then be 'transmitted' on an unpitched percussion instrument such as a small drum. The code could begin by being no more than the number of letters in a pupil's name: so to transmit the name JOHN SMITH, the player beats 4 beats, followed by a short pause, followed by 5 beats.

Such an exercise may seem trivial, but it immediately obliges pupils to listen carefully, if only to count the number of beats being played. It also demands careful and accurate playing of those same beats, and thus incorporates the two essential aspects of rhythm (and indeed music) education, namely *performance* and *listening*, into an activity which can also be great fun.

A development of this simple beginning would be the use of names of football teams to make up a 'news item', consisting of football results. Names of teams can be transmitted in the same way that names of pupils were, and then after a suitable rhythmic signal the score could be beaten out: 'Arsenal 1; Leyton Orient 4' would then become 7 beats, followed by an appropriate signal and then 1 beat, followed by 6 beats, a short pause, another 6 beats, the signal and 4 beats. Already this is rather more complicated than just transmitting names, and a certain amount of accuracy as well as patience will be required from the pupils, especially if groups of them are playing in unison, perhaps with a conductor.

A further development of this idea is the use of an *indirect* code, where a name is represented not by the number of its letters made into beats, but by a previously arranged and known rhythmic idea. For example:

Arsenal = $\frac{3}{4}$ 𝅘𝅥𝅭 𝅘𝅥𝅮 𝅘𝅥 | Manchester United = $\frac{4}{4}$ 𝅗𝅥 𝅘𝅥 𝅘𝅥 |

This is not only considerably harder for pupils, but can also introduce conventional notation into the exercise, since both 'transmitters' and 'receivers' would need a written reminder of the code if it extended beyond more than a very few teams. A slightly easier idea would be to take the rhythmic idea from the natural rhythm of the team's name, so that:

This is of course an extension of one of Carl Orff's ideas.

Clearly the Jungle telegraph project does not have to consist purely of football results. Indeed any information would be perfectly valid, and should perhaps depend only on what is likely to interest and motivate the pupils. For example, with very young children movement could also be incorporated into this exercise. Coded messages could be given to trigger a physical response: 'lift up your arm', 'stand up', 'touch the floor', etc. Another possibility with older children is the use of their telephone numbers (real or imaginary) with a Jungle telegraph system of 'phoning up' another pupil, using a rhythmic system of dialling.

PROJECT 2

Extended rhythm squares

Although the idea of the rhythm square is not new, it does have one or two distinct advantages over other forms of rhythmic exercise. First, the rhythms denoted are easily assimilated by the player, regardless of his or her knowledge of conventional notation. In fact rhythm squares may be used before, as a preliminary to, or after conventional notation.

Secondly, the square allows an early progression to the playing of complex rhythms and rhythmic counterpoints, precisely because it does not rely on a form of notation which would almost certainly make such work inaccessible to most pupils. Thirdly, rhythm squares are far more creative than conventional exercises, because of the flexibility of the system of notation, the possibilities for interpretation which they present to pupils, and also because pupils can easily construct their own rhythm squares.

The squares consist of a grid, in which smaller squares are filled with either single beats (●), pairs of beats (2) or triplets (3). Each small square represents the same basic time value, similar to a bar of music, and the rhythm square can then be 'played', using simple instruments.

There are many ways in which this can be done. The most obvious is from left to right, starting with the top line and working downwards, as one would read a book or an ordinary piece of music. Here is an example, with its top line also printed in conventional notation:

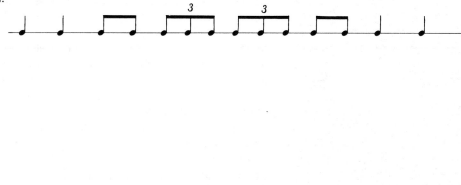

•	•	2	3	3	2	•	•
•	2	3			3	2	•
2	•		•	•		•	2
3		•	2	2	•		3
3		•	2	2	•		3
2	•		•	•		•	2
•	2	3			3	2	•
•	•	2	3	3	2	•	•

There are of course alternatives to such an obvious realization of the rhythm square. One pattern could be read like Chinese writing, moving downwards in rows starting from the extreme right of the pattern. Alternatively it could be read backwards starting from the bottom of the square, or perhaps in chain formation as follows:

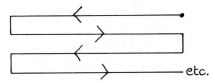

Brian Dennis

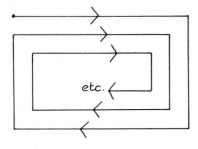

Diminishing squares spiralling

A series of diminishing squares ('spiralling') might provide yet another intriguing route to follow:

It is obviously best to start this work in unison in class, in order to get the rhythmic patterns accurately played, but once this has been achieved there are several ways in which any number of different players or groups can play in counterpart with each other. (With a full class the teacher should probably limit the number of groups to four!)

The simplest canon would be achieved by the first group playing the first line twice, followed by the second group, and so on. Alternatively each group could begin together, but from different parts of the rhythm square, such as the four corners:

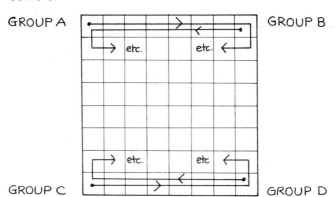

The four groups could then start together or enter in canon. Spiralling would also be possible in canon, starting from the same or different corners.

When playing in groups it is a good idea for each one to have its own instrumental character, always remembering that the instruments used should be non-pitched percussion ones. The low cost of these obviously makes this kind of work most suitable with whole classes in schools, giving everyone a chance to participate.

The following rhythm squares, rectangles (and a staircase!) are all based on the principle of the rhythm squares outlined above. They introduce the idea of bars within the rhythm square and also complex 'time signatures'. While teachers may not wish to use them all, the material is in fact suitable for primary to HE level, depending on the speed at which they are taken and the combination of groups and players used.

Simple systems

1st dot machine

$\frac{3}{4}$ double line clearly indicating the division into groups of three. This would obviously be played left to right, top to bottom.

2nd dot machine

$\frac{3}{4}$ as above but with syncopation

Criss-cross machine

$\frac{3}{4}$ playable left to right, top to bottom
top to bottom, left to right
bottom to top, left to right
right to left, top to bottom, etc.

$2 = $ ♫

The procession of 4-legged robots

$\frac{4}{4}$ playable left to right, top to bottom
right to left, top to bottom

Moon control
4/4 syncopated

The radar scanner
4/4 with ●, 2 and 3

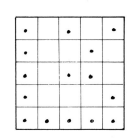

5-star robots
5/4 in complex bar lengths

1   2   3

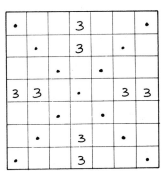

The X-machine
Play the dots and 3s on different instruments

The 7-star scanner

The 7:5 scanner

A staircase of wheels

Further developments of these ideas are possible, and individual teachers will be able to adapt them to suit their own requirements. For example, when copying out the grids for class use, different colours could be used for the dots or numbers in the grids, to represent the different instruments that could be played. Also, pupils can develop their own rhythm squares, having been given their own 'quota' of dots (for example 6 dots, 6 2s and 6 3s, etc.).

Finally, it is even possible to play a form of musical 'battleships', using a grid where a previously arranged rhythmic idea represents a battleship, another a destroyer, another a frigate, etc. One group plays the prepared grid to the other group, whose members only have an empty grid in front of them which they follow in the pre-arranged direction of the playing group. Whenever the battleship or other appropriate 'motif' occurs, the second group has to identify the square in which it was played, thus scoring a 'hit' whenever the pupils are correct. Any ships which were not identified during the performance were not 'sunk'!

The teacher can of course control the degree of difficulty in this game. Obviously it is much easier if the pulse is given or the rhythm is counted. It may be particularly difficult if the receiving group is not allowed to watch while the sending group is conducted by a silent beat (after an audible bar-for-nothing to set the pace and define the first beat). This could be quite a challenge even for able pupils!

Books and articles by the same author

Experimental Music in Schools OUP, 1970
Projects in Sound Universal Edition, 1975
'Experimental School Music' in *Musical Times*, August 1972
'Experimental School Music' in *International Music Educator*, 1972
'Guidelines for the development of creative music in education' in *Music in Education*, October 1978

Listening to music

Roy Bennett

Music 'appreciation' is not a fashionable aspect of secondary school music. It has been ignored by almost all those who have produced recent new ideas in music education, and for many teachers it conjures up images of their own past endurance tests in the classroom, listening to the works of the great masters.

Yet the sales of Roy Bennett's books Enjoying Music, *which are designed to accompany music appreciation work in schools, suggest that whatever the 'experts' say, music appreciation is still going on in a great many schools. Many teachers will therefore find Roy Bennett's four projects very useful, not only in themselves, but also as a guide to the planning of a programme of music listening.*

Roy Bennett has found that the best listening lessons result from the use of exclusively taped music. This makes for smoother 'stage managing' of the lesson by making all extracts available at the touch of a button; it avoids the embarrassment of 'missing' the start of a track when using a stylus and record player; and it also has the very positive advantage of enabling the teacher to improve the quality of a recording, by filtering out surface noise or brightening a dim-sounding recording. Perhaps most important of all, structured lesson material is preserved for future use.

However, taping records or music from the radio does raise problems of mechanical copyright, and music teachers should establish exactly what their legal position is before attempting to start any such recording. *The Mechanical-Copyright Protection Society (380 Streatham High Road, London SW16) will provide advice on this. Teachers can also contact their own education authority, who may already hold a 'blanket' licence for recording music in schools.*

PROJECT 1

The 'ingredients' which make up a piece of music

This is suggested as a 'lead-in' lesson, with the material treated initially at a rather basic level, leaving possibilities for further exploration later.

Approach

Make the point that when a composer writes a piece of music he or she is mixing together several musical ingredients. This information may be put on a worksheet:

Melody: perhaps the most important ingredient of all
Harmony: chords – two or more notes played at the same time
Beat: regular, steady pulse
Rhythm: irregular – often more exciting than beat alone
Timbre: the special sound, or 'tone-colour', of an instrument or group of instruments

---

Practical illustration

Discuss and demonstrate each of these musical ingredients separately, using a well-known tune, for example *Eye Level*, the theme from the television series *Van der Valk* (sheet music published by De Wolfe Ltd; record: Columbia DB 8946).

1. **Melody:** play the melodic line only, on the piano.
2. **Harmony:** add a simple harmonic framework by sketching basic chords here and there, but taking care not to emphasize beat or rhythm as yet.

3. **Beat:** play the melody above steady pulsing chords – one chord to each crotchet beat.
4. **Rhythm:** free the texture by allowing the melody now to ride above a relaxed, rhythmic accompaniment.
5. **Timbre:** play a recording of the tune in its original orchestration.

Further illustrations

(In each of the following, A is taken from the record 'Sir Adrian Boult introduces the Instruments of the Orchestra' (CFP 40074) so that each instrument is first heard without orchestral accompaniment; B is taken from a complete recording of the appropriate piece.)

1A **Melody only:** cor anglais (darkish timbre) – *Largo* from Dvořák's *'New World' Symphony*
1B **Melody + harmony:** cor anglais plays the melody; strings and low woodwind supply the harmony
2A **Melody only:** piccolo (bright timbre) – from the Overture to *Semiramide*, by Rossini
2B **Melody + harmony + beat:** woodwind instruments take the melody; the rest of the orchestra supplies the harmony – and a steady beat
3A **Melody only** – but a melody that is itself very rhythmic: piccolo and oboe (a mixture of timbres) – from the Overture to *The Silken Ladder*, by Rossini
3B **Melody + harmony + rhythm + timbre:** the melody is played twice – the second time by a quite different combination of instruments. This change in orchestration presents a variety of timbres:
   1. melody – violins; rhythm – plucked double basses
   2. melody – piccolo and oboe; rhythm and harmony – other woodwinds

Follow-up

Play short, well-varied extracts of music, with key questions to test understanding. Some examples:

A The toreador's march section from Bizet's Prelude to *Carmen*
   1. Which do you think is most important in this music – beat, or rhythm?
   2. Which section of the orchestra is supplying it?
   3. Which instruments are playing the melody?
B Opening of the slow movement from Symphony No. 5, by Tchaikovsky
   1. Which is more important here – rhythm, or melody?
   2. Which instrument supplies it?
   3. Choose a word to describe the timbre of this instrument.
   4. Which section of the orchestra is playing the harmony?
C Title-music from the film: *The Magnificent Seven*
   1. Which is most important in this music – beat, or rhythm?
   2. Which two sections of the orchestra are supplying it?
   3. Which instruments play the melody?

PROJECT 2

Timbre and texture in music

This takes the investigation of timbre a little further, and attempts to link it with some understanding of texture in music, using the senses of sight and touch as well as hearing. For this lesson, pieces of various kinds of fabric are needed:

tweed: a mixture of colours offering a soft, muted effect – 'quiet' blues, greens, mauves

cotton: vividly printed in clashing colours – reds, purples, pinks, oranges
velvet: rich, warm and dark in colour
hessian: rough, coarse, but brightly coloured
lace: as fine, delicate and intricate as possible

It can, of course, be argued that linking colour with music has its dangers, particularly if specific colours are matched to individual instruments. However, the intention here is merely to point out similarities in quality and effect between combinations of colours and combinations of sounds: bright or dark, vivid or muted, clashing or blending. Using the coloured fabrics in the lesson, especially if members of the class are encouraged to touch them to appreciate the differing textures, stimulates interest and curiosity, and offers an incentive to more alert listening.

The lesson might be presented to the class in the following way:

Timbre

Each instrument has its own special sound. The characteristic sound of a trumpet, for instance, makes it possible for us to recognize it; to tell the difference between the sound of a trumpet and, say, a violin. We call this special sound, the *timbre* of the instrument.

(Illustrate with tape-recorded snatches of various instruments: trumpet, violin, piccolo, bassoon, each heard unaccompanied. Discuss, and compare, the characteristic timbres of these instruments.)

Combinations of timbres
(Show, and discuss, the colour-effects, blending and clashing of the tweed and cotton.)
A composer can *blend* the timbres of certain instruments.
(Play the Death of Åse from *Peer Gynt*, by Grieg)
Grieg scores this music for strings only: instruments of the same type whose timbres blend together, rather like the soft blending of related colours in the piece of tweed.

But a composer may choose to *contrast* the timbres of different instruments to produce a colourful, clashing effect:
(Play Kastchei's Dance from *The Firebird*, by Stravinsky)
In this piece, Stravinsky deliberately combines instruments whose timbres are sharply contrasted, producing colourful, clashing sounds, like a fabric printed in vivid, clashing colours.

Texture

(Show the velvet, hessian and lace. Discuss the texture of each fabric.)
Some pieces of music have a smooth, flowing sound. Others may sound rough, jagged, spiky. We call this aspect of a piece of music the *texture* of the music.
(Play the opening of the slow movement of Beethoven's Piano Concerto No. 5, 'Emperor')
We can compare the texture of this music with that of a piece of velvet. Some words might describe the texture of both: soft, rich, smooth, flowing, warm.
(Play the Storm Interlude from *Peter Grimes*, by Britten)
In this music, the texture is more like a piece of hessian: rough, harsh, coarse.
(Play an intricate but lightly textured harpsichord sonata by Scarlatti)
The texture of this music is light and open, delicate and intricate, like a piece of fine lace.

Follow-up

1. Using the same fabrics, or a selection of other kinds, play further extracts of music for the class to match both the timbres and the texture of each piece with one of the fabrics shown.
2. Select other extracts of music for the children to describe in their own words (*without* the aid of fabrics) the timbres and texture presented in each piece.

3. Further follow-up work, often with very interesting results, could involve liaison with the Art department. After hearing a particularly vivid orchestral piece (for example, Khachaturian's *Sabre Dance*) several times, each member of the class paints or colours an abstract picture, or creates a collage, to parallel his impressions of the timbres and textures presented in the music.

PROJECT 3

Music and coloured slides

This lesson is a suggested approach with groups where concentration may be poor. In such situations it might be advisable to devote no more than half a lesson to listening, filling the remainder with other musical activities.

For this lesson, a handful of coloured slides of varied content are needed, and for each slide, two carefully chosen extracts of music recorded onto tape. The intention is to provide interest by means of visual stimulus, and so provoke reaction in the form of discussion or some kind of written response.

In some of the pairs of extracts, one piece of music matches the slide to be shown; the other does not. For example:

Slide bleak, snow-covered, northern landscape
Music A Vaughan Williams: *Sinfonia Antartica*
Music B Massenet: Castillane, from *Le Cid*

Discuss which music best matches the picture shown. Ask what musical 'clues' the music provides. (In the case of a musically inexperienced group, a selection of such clues might be written on the blackboard at the beginning of the lesson, including: choice of instruments; speed; dynamics; rhythms; harmonies; texture.)

In other pairs of extracts, each piece may be specifically intended by its composer to convey aspects portrayed in the slide to be shown:

Slide stormy sea
Music A Britten: Storm Interlude from *Peter Grimes*
Music B Wagner: Overture to *The Flying Dutchman*

Discussion here would centre around which composer paints the most vivid and convincing sound-picture. Do not be discouraged should any members of the class obstinately insist that neither piece really matches! Ask them to explain what, in their opinion, is lacking, and what the music *should* be like. (Disagreement with the 'right' piece is not too important – the fact that they are actually discussing the music has its own value.)

A third way of pairing extracts is with the intention that either will match the slide, according to two possible interpretations. The point should be raised here that music can, in fact, 'colour' our interpretation of what we see, evoking emotion or suggesting information which the picture may not in itself make clear. An example:

Slide village nestling in peaceful valley; serene mountains
Music A Prokofiev: Romeo at Juliet's before Parting, from *Romeo and Juliet* (Suite 2, No. 5)
Music B Holst: Mars, the Bringer of War, from *The Planets*

Interpreting literally what the eye sees, Music A matches perfectly. But if we imagine this to be a 'still' from a war film, Music B might be equally appropriate (perhaps suggesting that within seconds, fighter aircraft will zoom down between the mountains and obliterate the village with bomb-blast).

PROJECT 4

Appreciation in detail

A suggested structure for a listening lesson based upon a single piece: Montagues and Capulets, from the ballet *Romeo and Juliet* by Prokofiev (Suite 2, No. 1. Recording: Supraphon SUAST 50104)

Lesson material

1 Find pictures from a production of *Romeo and Juliet*, showing key events in the story, especially encounters between the two rival families.
2 'Montagues and Capulets' is in ternary form (A¹ B A²) prefaced by a slow introduction. Record, separately, on tape:
   1. the introduction
   2. section A¹
   3. section B
   4. section A²
   5. section B, again
   6. the piece complete

Approach

1 Give brief details of the life and music of Prokofiev.
2 Outline the story of Romeo and Juliet, showing pictures of scenes.
3 Explain 'ballet', emphasizing the more vigorous, dramatic qualities of many 20th-century ballets.
4 Familiarize the children with the main tunes (A and B below) by playing them two or three times each on the piano. Mention (or better still, draw from members of the class) the more obvious points of musical contrast between them:
   Tune A: *forte*, strong and rhythmic, striding, aggressive
   Tune B: *piano*, more moderate in speed, peaceful and flowing
   (The children should be able to see the tunes, either in print, or written out on the blackboard.)
5 Explain how Prokofiev designs this piece in ternary form (a 'musical sandwich') but with a mood-setting introduction. Draw a simple diagram on the blackboard to make this clear, pointing out that the first and last sections (A) of the ternary design use the same music; the middle section (B) presents a contrast.

Listening

Play the music on tape, *in sections* (recording 1–4, above). The following description could be part of an accompanying worksheet:
1 A short but powerfully dramatic introduction: a deafening *crescendo* of harsh chords with rolls on cymbals and drums suddenly dissolving into hushed chords for muted strings. This is repeated.
2 A strong rhythm begins. Above this strides a tune (A) which suggests the arrogant swagger of the Montagues and Capulets.

3 The music of the middle section (B) presents a contrast, and is mainly for woodwind instruments.

4 Then the powerful, striding music returns to end the piece.

The music should be played again, in sections (recordings 1–4, repeated). Focus concentration by setting simple questions, giving the class something to listen *for*:

1 (a) Name some of the instruments which build up the harsh chords.
   (b) Which drums play the 'rolls' in this introduction?
2 (a) Which instruments play the striding tune of Music A?
   (b) Name another kind of drum heard in this section of the piece.
3 (a) Which woodwind instrument plays Tune B the first time we hear it?
   (b) When Tune B is repeated, which instruments weave quiet patterns high in the background?
4 (a) Which instruments play the first phrases of the striding tune when Music A returns to end the piece?
   (b) Does the music end loudly, or quietly? What is the Italian word for this?
5 Listen again to the contrasting middle section of the piece, and make a list of the percussion instruments you recognize. (Recording 5)

The piece is now heard complete (played as many times as necessary) while some or all of the following work is tackled:
1 Make a list of the musical contrasts you notice when Music A is followed by Music B.
2 When Music A returns to end the piece, is it the same as it was at first – or does Prokofiev make any important changes?
3 Make up a diagram of your own, showing how a composer builds up a piece in *Ternary form*. Colour or shade in different ways the sections of your diagram which represent Music A and Music B, to give a clear idea of the musical contrasts between them.

Further follow-up might consist of factual or imaginative writing or drawing, evaluating the children's response to the music and its background.

Suggestions for further listening

1 One or two other pieces from Prokofiev's *Romeo and Juliet*: 'Masks' (also in ternary form); 'Death of Tybalt' (strong imaginative-pictorial background)
2 More music by Prokofiev: 'Sleigh Ride' from *Lieutenant Kije*; Gavotte from the Classical Symphony
3 Other musical versions of the story of Romeo and Juliet: Tchaikovsky (Fantasy-Overture); Bernstein: *West Side Story*
4 Dances from other 20th-century ballets: The Miller's Dance from *The Three-Cornered Hat*, by Falla; Kastchei's Dance from *The Firebird*, by Stravinsky; Hoe-Down from *Rodeo*, by Copland

Related bibliography

D. Jenkins and M. Visocchi: *Portraits in Music* (Books 1 and 2) OUP
   Two books containing over 30 suggestions for listening, ranging from popular programme music to some 20th-century music which may be new to the classroom repertoire.

R. Bennett: *Enjoying Music* (Books 1–3) Longman
   Each book contains twenty or more pieces, ranging from the 13th to the 20th centuries, offering a basis for listening lessons. A series of workbooks containing follow-up ideas is also available.

© Roy Bennett

Indian music

Leela Floyd

During the last 20 years our school population, particularly in inner-city areas, has brought new cultures into our classrooms. The existence of large numbers of certain ethnic groups in some schools has presented a challenge to traditional teaching methods and curricula, which has already been faced in several earlier chapters of this book.

But while many teachers may find African, Reggae or Steelband music relatively easy to deal with in schools, Asian music has always remained very much on the outskirts of the classroom, surrounded by an aura of mystery. Admittedly it is a difficult task to incorporate Asian music into the general music syllabus, because it is based on a totally different system from that in the West; but the educational and social reasons for attempting to do so are surely very strong.

In compressing centuries of musical development into ordinary music lessons, Leela Floyd is only too aware of the problems that this poses (which are similar to those faced by Michael Burnett with early music):

'My answer is a simple one which may evoke some criticism from oriental scholars, experts and armchair theorists; but they cannot necessarily solve our present classroom problems. My belief is that a modest understanding of "other" music coupled with a genuine sympathy and interest are all that a music teacher needs to tackle this kind of work.'

Teachers should therefore not feel that this chapter is not for them, simply because they do not feel 'qualified' to deal with Indian music. Leela Floyd has suggested a number of basic activities which are musically simple, and could be the basis for much interesting work in the classroom. Her ideas are preceded by a short and helpful summary of the elements of Indian music.

An introduction to Indian music

Before describing the practical work and listening suggestions in this chapter, most readers will benefit from a brief introducton to the three main elements in Indian music.

Drone

Many newcomers to Indian music comment on the strange and hypnotic sound of the drone. All Indian music is played or sung to a drone, but it takes some time before one can learn to appreciate its function, and listen to the melody and rhythm that goes on behind it. The drone is an unconscious source of harmony in Indian music.

Performances usually have one drone player but in some cases there may be two musicians playing the drone. For example in a **shehnai** (a double-reeded wind instrument similar to the oboe) performance the drone may be played by two or even three shenais sounding rather like a bagpipe drone. The drone notes are usually tuned to the tonic (often an octave apart) and the fourth or fifth note below the tonic note. Most performances begin with the drone notes which are played continuously throughout the performance, providing a constant reminder of the tonic to the main soloist.

A drone instrument

The **tambura** is the most commonly used drone instrument. It is a long-necked stringed instrument with four strings and at one end a large gourd. The player holds the tambura upright with the gourd resting on his lap. The notes are strummed continuously one after another, creating a hypnotic effect on the listener.

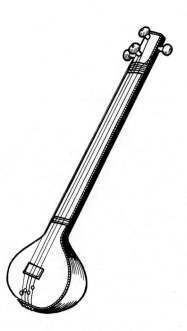

Tala

Perhaps the most complex aspect of Indian music lies in the **tala** or time cycle.

The tala provides the rhythmic background to the whole performance. Each performance is set to a tala and a **laya** (or tempo). Individual talas have special characteristics and may be divided into various groups of time units or **matras** (beats). An ancient Hindu treatise on music describes the tala in the following way:

> 'Tala is like the body of a man in which matras (beats) are like arteries, laya (tempo) is like blood flowing in them and strokes (drum strokes) are like the various limbs.'

There are hundreds of talas and each **tabla** (drum) player has to memorize a complex system of basic rhythms with the help of mnemonic syllables called **bols**. Each syllable will indicate what and how to play on the drums. Each tala is like a repeated rhythmic pattern which is played in a cycle with intricate variations. But perhaps the most exciting part of the tala is that after every rhythmic invention within the time cycle, the performer must always return in time to the **sam** or first beat.

A rhythmic instrument

The **tabla** is the most popular instrument used for rhythmic accompaniment. It is a pair of drums, a wooden treble drum and a bass metal drum. The right-hand or treble drum is usually tuned to the tonic and the left-hand or bass drum is often tuned a fourth or fifth below the treble drum.

Raga

There is no conscious harmony in Indian music as there is in western music, but Indian music is centred around melody, which through the centuries has become an intricate and refined art. Since there was no notation in Indian music, as in the western sense, each melody and melodic style was passed on orally from father to son and Guru to pupil, in an atmosphere of utmost secrecy. It would be impossible to explain all the intricate aspects of the **raga** and the following is therefore a very limited and simple explanation.

Every performance is based on a chosen raga or fixed melodic composition. Each raga portrays a particular emotion and mood which is developed and explained through the artistry of the individual soloist. Ragas are also associated with seasons, colours, visual images and times of the day (dawn, noon, midnight, etc.). Each performance of a raga is an attempt to express feelings at a given moment through the character and rules of the chosen raga and tala. The emotive power of the music will be based on the way in which four main notes of each raga are emphasized and woven into melodies and their variations. These four notes are called the **Vadi** (chief note), **Samvadi** (supporting note), **Anuvadi** (complementary note) and **Vivadi** (discordant note).

A melodic instrument

The **sitar** is perhaps the most commonly used melodic instrument of northern India. It resembles the tambura (drone instrument) and has seven melody strings which are plucked with a wire plectrum. Underneath the main strings are about 19 strings which vibrate in sympathy with the playing of the other strings. There are 20 movable frets of curved brass along the neck of the sitar, which can be easily adjusted to suit the various raga scales to be played.

Practical projects

It would be impossible to re-create the exact sound and mood of Indian music, particularly on traditional classroom instruments. Therefore I can only advise teachers to experiment and improvise on the ideas in the projects according to their individual situation and their vision of Indian music.

Preliminary points

Instruments

One can use a great variety of instruments depending on what is available. It is naturally better to have a contrast of sound colours wherever possible, and in general it would be a good idea to choose instruments with sustaining power to play the drone and the melody. The tala would be easier to play on percussion instruments such as the bongo, castanets or maracas. If there are pupils who can play any orchestral or ethnic instrument it may be an ideal opportunity to explore more interesting sounds. Conventional instruments such as the piano and cello are useful for playing the drone in the lower register.

Seating

It may be more comfortable if children sit in a circle or in two semi-circles facing each other. Give each child an instrument if possible. Sometimes the class may be divided into smaller groups, such as the drone, tala and melody group. In this way the children may have greater freedom to learn their own parts and perhaps even bring new ideas into their creative activities.

Drone projects

The drone provides a basic ostinato rhythm for many of the projects. The drone notes may be repeated over and over again in the lower register while melodic and rhythmic patterns are played above it. A simple drone of two notes a fourth or fifth apart for example, played in crotchets on a bass xylophone or on the lower register of the piano, sounds particularly effective.

VARIATION 1
A drone can be sung or played like a round as seen below.

VARIATION 2
Playing a drone in contrary motion is another interesting device.

VARIATION 3
Repeating or echoing the notes of the drone on different registers is another possibility.

The variations are plentiful and teachers can therefore experiment with interesting and unusual possibilities.

Tala projects

The following talas may be said, clapped or played on percussion instruments. The X indicates the claps (or main beats) and the O shows the silent or rest beats. Always end each tala on the first beat of the next rhythmic cycle.

Bols

The rhythmic syllables or *bols* may present a problem to those who cannot pronounce them or maintain a consistent rhythmic lilt. However, it is worth the effort to try and work them out with the help of any pupils in the class who may understand the sounds. The syllables *Dha* and *Dhin* are pronounced with a heavy accent on the *Dh. Ti, na, ta, trik* and *din*, are said exactly as they are written. *Gé* is heavily accentuated. The main thing to remember is to try and maintain a steady rhythm right through the tala.

Some talas

1. *Dadara* (6 time units)

Dha	Dhin	Dha	Dha	Ti	Na ——→	Dha
1	2	3	4	5	6	1
X			0			X

2. *Rupaka* (7 time units)

Dha	Dha	Trik	Dhin	Dhin	Dha	Trik ——→	Dha
1	2	3	4	5	6	7	1
X			X		X		X

3. *Jhapatala* (10 time units)

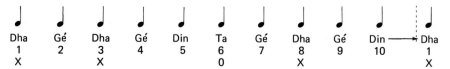

Dha	Gé	Dha	Gé	Din	Ta	Gé	Dha	Gé	Din ——→	Dha
1	2	3	4	5	6	7	8	9	10	1
X		X			0		X			X

VARIATION 1

The syllables can also be transferred into instruments to create a pattern of rhythmic sounds as shown in the project below.

Dadara tala (6 time units)

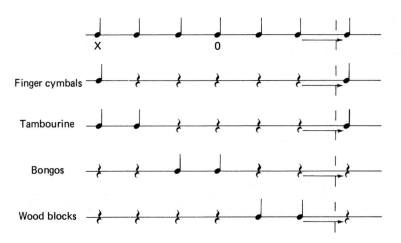

VARIATION 2

Talas may also be played or spoken above a continuous drone as shown below.

Rupaka (7 time units)

Raga projects

Here is a selection of ragas which portray different moods. Each raga has its own ascending and descending scale pattern. Each also has its drone notes which in the ragas mentioned are also the main notes of the raga.

1. *Ananda Bhairava (after sunrise)* Joyful and energetic mood
drone notes – C & F

2. *Bhimapalashri (early afternoon)* Tender and pleasing mood
drone notes – F & C

3. *Dipaka (after sunset)* Fiery and vigorous mood
drone notes – G & C

VARIATION 1
Classes may be divided in two groups, where one plays the ascending scale and the other follows with the descending pattern. This may be repeated high/low or loud/soft on a selection of instruments. The piano creates an interesting framework for the scale patterns by playing the drone notes in the bass with the pedal down.

VARIATION 2
As children get more used to the sound of the scale patterns they may create short, decorative phrases around the main notes as shown below. The tune is based on the notes of *Raga Malkosh*.

Night Raga Peaceful mood
main notes – E & B

VARIATION 3
One simple way of improvising is to repeat a written tune based on the notes of the raga. Each repetition or phrase may be played slightly differently in a number of ways as in the example overleaf.

Raga Bhupali (night) Harmonious and contented mood

Listening to Indian music

Music appreciation is probably one of the unique areas of the curriculum where pupils of all abilities and backgrounds have the opportunity to share an aesthetic experience. It is this rare quality about music that can move children and adults into experiencing 'non-worldly' spheres. The ancient Hindus had a special term to describe this profound musical experience, *rasa*, or quintessence.

A musical score is an invaluable aid to learning about written music, but another way of learning is to listen to unwritten improvised music as in some jazz, blues or Indian music. Since Indian music is centred around a mood it can have a distinct psychological effect on the listener. In descriptive western music, such as *Peter and the Wolf* or *The Sorcerer's Apprentice*, teachers usually underline the story; but in Indian music this is not possible. When a *raga* is being played or sung, a visual picture is formed according to its emotional qualities. Of course, these images will vary according to one's own mood, and it would not be possible to give any literal translation of a raga. But there are many Indian paintings which powerfully describe the sentiments, moods and seasons of certain *ragas*. Looking at these paintings does have the merit of helping us to understand how artists of the time interpreted some of this music. For example, *Raga Megha* is shown to portray a dynamic figure seated on an elephant and *Raga Basant* shows a beautiful youth decked in flowers. Some of the greatest of these paintings can be seen in the famous *Ragamala* collection, illustrations of which can be purchased in most oriental book shops.

Some suggestions

Before introducing an Indian music performance to a class, it may be a good idea to trace how Indian music came to the west. One way is to point out the use of the *sitar, tabla* or any other Indian instrument that was recorded in some pop songs. A lesson on pop (see pages 52 to 58) may therefore include some of these examples, so that pupils can see how Indian music has influenced famous pop stars.

Most children are usually surprised to hear an Indian instrument or tune in a western pop song. The music of The Beatles, Pink Floyd, Indo Jazz Fusions, Third Ear Band, Quintessence, Alice Coltrane, Terry Riley and many others have shown Indian influences, but it was The Beatles and Yehudi Menuhin who helped to bring it to a wider and varied audience in the early 60s. Here are a few examples from western pop:

Within you, without you, from The Beatles' LP, *Sergeant Pepper's Lonely Hearts' Club Band* has *tabla* accompaniment, *sarangi* (stringed Indian instrument) and drone. (Parlophone PCS 7027)
Paint it Black, no. 1 in the charts in 1966, by the Rolling Stones has a *sitar* playing.
My Sweet Lord, no. 1 in the charts in 1971, by George Harrison. The chorus backing is sung in Hindu religious words. (Apple Records)

Here are some examples of contemporary serious musicians and their Indian music influences.

Terry Riley's LP, *Rainbow in Curved Air*. The music has repeated phrases played on keyboard instruments which are based on the Indian *tala* system. (CBS 64564)
Alan Hovhaness's LP, *Fantasy for Piano*. The composer used Indian modes and rhythms.
John McLaughlin's LP, *Shakti*. A combination of guitar with Indian violin. (CBS 81388)

Here are examples of Indian music recordings which may also be used for listening. Most children will not be able to take in a whole LP at a time, and it would therefore be advisable to begin with shorter recordings and go on to the longer ones. Each LP cover will usually give a brief note on the music and the musician which is quite helpful.

Ustad Ali Akbar Khan (Sarod), EMI D/ELRZ 8; side 2: Raga Malkauns.
A pentatonic raga which is played fairly simply in this recording. The main tune is easily recognizable and is played over and over again throughout the performance. The mood is meant to convey prayer, peacefulness and meditation. It is usually played at midnight, though many modern musicians play it at other times of the day. The drone is an unusual one.
Shivkumar Sharma (Santoor), EMI ECSD 2389. Side 1 of Raga Malkauns is treated differently from the performance above.
Ravi Shankar improvisations, Liberty LBL 83076E. Side 1 has music from the well-known Indian movie by Satyajit Ray, *Panther Panchali*.
Ustad Bismillah Khan (Shehnai), EMI LKDR 11; side 1. It is worth comparing the performance of the Raga Malkauns with the performances above.

The rest of the performances in each record are also worth listening to!

Related bibliography

The rhythmic and melodic variations on the *ragas* and *talas* of Indian music are unending, and teachers who wish to will find further examples in the following books:
L. Floyd: *Indian music* OUP, 1980 (with cassette)
    A book giving all the necessary information to teachers and pupils wanting to make a start on Indian music. With many photographs and practical projects recorded on cassette.

A. Danielou: *The ragas of North Indian Music* Barrie and Rockliff
F. Strangways: *The Music of Hindostan* Clarendon Press (Oxford), 1965
P. Holroyde: *Indian Music* Allen & Unwin, 1972
R. Shankar: *My music, my life* Jonathan Cape, 1969

© Leela Floyd

Recording and electronics in the classroom

Peter West

This final chapter has three main aims. The first is to give teachers general advice about starting or further developing classroom work in recording and electronics. (Advice is particularly important in an area which embraces so many different types and makes of equipment.) Secondly, there are several ideas suggested for classroom activities which will be possible in many schools and which need not involve a great amount of equipment. Lastly, this chapter is intended to encourage an overall strategy and integrated approach to using recording and electronic equipment in schools. Peter West describes this strategy as 'building a sound resource centre'.

Working with tape recorders and even quite sophisticated electronic equipment, such as the synthesizer, is not of course new. Many teachers have been working in this area for a long time, and while there has been a lot of success for some, others have found themselves wandering from one novelty to the next, not always knowing why they are using the equipment, except perhaps to try to tame unruly classes for whom music has previously had little to offer.

Unfortunately the shallowness of this approach soon becomes evident: what do you do when the kids get bored with the school's brand new synthesizer after a couple of 'lessons' on it? Peter West's following suggestions should help to provide the answer. They will also show that a lot of exciting work can be done without ever using anything as complicated and expensive as a synthesizer.

A sound resource centre

The idea of a *sound resource centre* may seem strange at first, yet in the visual sense a resource centre is of course something with which many pupils are already familiar. It is commonplace to find one in a school, often based round a library which houses pictures, slides, leaflets, etc., which the pupils are encouraged to use in order to help in particular projects. Why not have the same idea in music, where particular sounds or musical ideas are stored on recording tape?

Ideally pupils would have blank cassettes allotted to them which they could use with cassette recorders. Then, whether they recorded outside or inside school, with chime bars or synthesizer, those cassettes with 'worthwhile' sounds could be stored for future use: for example, in the creation of a sound collage, or the treatment of the recording by the synthesizer, or as background sound to drama activities. (The 'judging' of which tapes should be stored could itself provide useful lesson material, but obviously this is a procedure which teachers would need to treat with some sensitivity.) For this kind of work it is very useful to have short two- or three-minute cassettes to store each sound separately. (See resource section, page 110.)

Throughout the following sections there are references to this idea of a sound resource unit. Whether such a unit is seen as being solely for the music department, or as an aid to storing interesting sounds for the whole school (as a kind of sound library), it will give the recording and electronic work of a music department some kind of common purpose.

Tape recorders

Equipment

A lot of what you *do* in the area of music teaching and electronics obviously depends on what you *have* in the way of equipment. This is particularly so in the case of tape recorders, since there are so many different sorts: reel-to-reel, cassette, mono, stereo, four-track, two-track, and so on. Music teachers often wonder what can be done with the various items that they acquire over the years, sometimes bought with no overall plan in mind, and they also want to know what new equipment to buy. There are really two aspects to these questions: compatibility and cost-effectiveness.

Whereas compatibility is not a problem with cassette machines, it can be something of a headache with the reel-to-reel recorder, especially when two machines are required for mixing and tracking. For example, four-track recorders cannot be used effectively with two-track ones, since the latter will simply play back two tracks at once (four if it is a stereo player!) with one of these (or two) reversed. So, if you want to buy a second tape recorder, you must ensure that it matches your present one's system of tracking.

All this of course assumes that you want to use reel-to-reel recorders. Most of the literature on tape work has dealt with these machines, not only because technically they are more versatile, but also because cassettes have only been available comparatively recently. Music teachers who were themselves brought up on reel-to-reel machines, and who rightly consider them superior in quality, have stuck to using them in the classroom.

Much of the conventional tape work has been done with small groups of pupils, perhaps sixth formers who have also had a scientific interest. These groups can be very successful, and teachers whose main concern is this kind of work will obviously find reel-to-reel machines their best buy, providing the advice above on tracking is followed. Reel-to-reel machines also have the very considerable advantage of offering potential in terms of tape speed change, which is never available on cassette machines of any price.

There are two further points about reel-to-reel tape recorders. First, four-track machines are perhaps to be avoided as a general rule. Secondly, cheap reel-to-reel machines are sometimes more complicated to use than the most expensive ones, and also demonstrate the advantages of reel-to-reel machines far less obviously. For teachers interested in reel-to-reel, it is best to buy a good quality two-track machine (since it is virtually impossible to reverse a four-track tape), or better still to buy *two* of these, in order to be able to build up several tracks of sound by using the two machines together. Since the bulk of educational literature available to teachers covers reel-to-reel machines (see resources section, page 110), no further suggestions will be made for them in this chapter.

However good reel-to-reel tape recorders are, it is difficult to see how whole classes of pupils can be easily occupied with just two or even three of them. Many teachers may therefore consider that cassette recorders would be a better buy, since several could be bought for the price of one reel-to-reel recorder. This could even mean that class sub-groups might be reduced to three or even two pupils per machine if the very cheapest models were purchased. Since there is nothing wrong with the cheaper machines, it is advisable to buy for quantity, not quality.

Using cassette machines

One of the greatest advantages with cassette record players, as well as their simplicity and portability, is their complete *interchangeability*. There is no problem about the number of tracks or mono/stereo compatibility. This means that although there will be obvious problems of synchronization, any amount of sound mixing can be achieved. Another advantage is that pupils are already so familiar with these machines that they will always find them easy to use.

Simple mixing
This can be achieved by using a minimum of three cassette machines. The mixing is done 'live' by simply playing two tapes, each through its own player, and recording both simultaneously on the third machine through a microphone. To anyone at all experienced in audio work this will seem crude, and likely to produce a final tape of poor quality, compared to connecting the machines *electrically* in order to do this. Nevertheless, there is the very real advantage that with audio mixing, pupils can hear throughout exactly what is happening, and this therefore makes the mixing process much easier to understand. It is also something that pupils can then do themselves, with the minimum of technical connections to go wrong.

This process of mixing obviously has a number of applications. For example, it can be used in 'creative' work, perhaps by building up a sound collage composition, using sounds which may have originated from the environment, from a synthesizer or even from tapes which came from the school's sound resource centre. Alternatively, the process can be used with conventional performance work, so that relatively able pupils can play simple duets 'with themselves' by recording both parts separately and trying to put them together in this way. There are of course synchronization difficulties, but a couple of pupils will find this problem an engaging one!

The environment project

One of the cassette recorder's advantages is its extreme portability, making outside work very easy, especially with machines that are fitted with internal microphones and automatic input volume controls. These have the advantages of mikes not being lost and recordings not being ruined by overloading. Recordings of sounds can be 'collected', taken back to school and listened to. Worthwhile ones can then be placed straight in the sound resource unit, used 'creatively' or in conjunction with an instrumental piece.

One project which has been successfully tried is making a sound 'map'. A group of pupils go out with as many cassette recorders as are available, together with a large map of the chosen area to be surveyed. Each pupil, or sub-group, is allotted a certain small area, and all the main sounds of that area are recorded, one after the other. Back in the classroom each pupil plots the sounds on his or her portion of the map, until the whole map has been completed.

This project can be done in a variety of ways. Perhaps the simplest is to indicate on the map the description of the sound. A further development would be to include an indication of the relative volume of each one. This can be quite difficult, especially when using automatic recorders, since each recording ends up at the same level. (When this particular project has been attempted, pupils themselves have developed a system of providing the recorder with a reference sound placed in front of the microphone, from which the volume of the sound being recorded can at least be estimated.) A further development of this project is to work in the area of sound 'pollution'. Here sounds are considered for their social acceptability, which is assessed and again plotted on a map.

For many music teachers this kind of work may seem rather far removed from the music lesson, though in fact a lot of interesting and useful work is provided back in school. The process of sifting through the recordings and comparing results can be an exercise in aural discrimination which is far more accessible and meaningful to pupils than traditional aural tests.

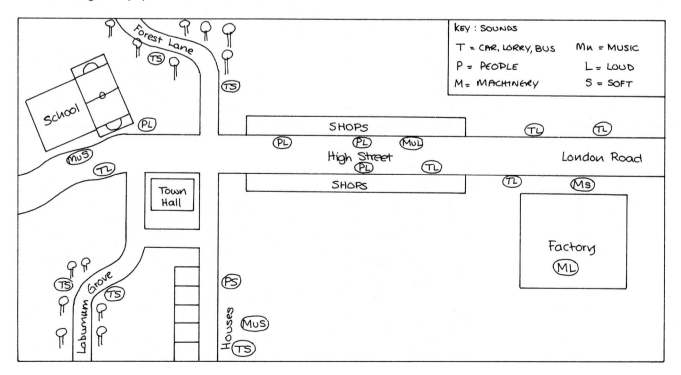

Using cassettes in the classroom

For teachers who prefer their pupils to be more obviously engaged in musical activities, there is a great deal that can be done with cassette recorders and conventional classroom instruments, such as chime bars and xylophones, and here there are particularly useful links with the idea of a sound resource unit.

The first approach in this area should be the recording of simple traditional musical ideas, which can then either be put together with several tape recorders, stored in the sound resource unit, or fed back into classroom instrument use. A good way to start is by recording a succession of identical simple chords (or a long sustained one if possible), so that several cassettes of the short type might each consist of simply related chords: one cassette might have two minutes of sustained C chord (a 'harmonic field'), another of F and a third of G. With two or more machines the chords could be put together to form a sequence, for example a backing tape of twelve-bar blues which a pupil can then use again in the classroom for improvisation.

Another possibility is to record similar pitches on one cassette, so that a collection of cassettes is built up, each containing a fairly random group of similar pitches. (The same could be done with similar tones.) A further development is to record cassettes of ostinati, each distinct in some way yet related to the others, which can again be mixed in a variety of ways, either with or without live performance.

The possibilities for using these taped results should not be underestimated. For example, the twelve-bar blues described above could easily be fed back into live classroom music for a singing lesson, where the class sing above their own tape of the accompaniment. In this way the potential of cassette tape working to augment and enrich normal practical work is fully exploited.

Synthesizers

This section has been put at the end of this chapter quite intentionally, to try to show that working with electronic equipment in schools does not *have* to mean using a synthesizer. All the work described above will, with the right approach and attitude, produce a huge amount of exciting and worthwhile activity without a school even thinking about buying a synthesizer. However, if a school does acquire or already own one, its work *may* certainly be enriched.

Which sort?

There are at present two categories of synthesizer. The first, which is made by EMS Ltd (see resource section, page 110) has no integrated keyboard, but produces its sounds by first placing electrical connecting pins in a *patchboard*. This type of synthesizer is useful for creative work, in that it can produce a great many science fiction type sounds, with a lot of patience and a certain amount of understanding from the user. However, since there is no constant tuning, even with the additional keyboard, the machine tends to be rather unmusical. Certainly it would be impossible to use as a melodic instrument in conjunction with other instruments.

This type of synthesizer is perhaps best used in a professional studio, where there is the experience and related equipment to obtain its full potential. In schools, its use is really restricted to very small groups of motivated and intelligent pupils, such as sixth formers. For younger pupils or larger groups the scientific and musical concepts are too demanding, and because the keyboard is not an integral part of the machine the access to sound is limited.

The second category of synthesizer does have an integral keyboard, and instead of having a system of pins in a patchboard to control the sounds, it has conventional controls. So the keyboard, which is always in tune (or can be immediately brought back to normal tuning) provides instant access to what the synthesizer can do, and this means that the equipment can be used in conjunction with other musical instruments. This type of synthesizer (which is produced by ARP, Moog, Yamaha, Roland and Sequential Circuits) can therefore be used with groups of pupils who are playing pop or traditional music. There are two types of keyboard synthesizer: monophonic and polyphonic. Most small 'lead' synthesizers are monophonic, and can therefore only play a single line of music. Polyphonic synthesizers have a number of 'voices', however, and of course it is important to find out just how many when purchasing. Both types of keyboard synthesizer can produce almost any sound and therefore imitate any solo instrument, while the polyphonic models have the advantage of being able to imitate a keyboard instrument – though they are very expensive pieces of equipment!

Synthesizers

with keyboard

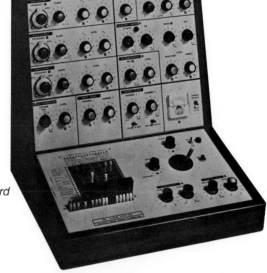

without keyboard

What can a synthesizer do?

As well as choosing the type of synthesizer, it is obviously important to find out what each individual model can do. The first comforting thought is that since synthesizers tend to be designed for aspiring but lazy or unmusical pop musicians, they always come supplied with operating manuals. Most also have some system of recording the control settings of each sound discovered by the user, so he or she can find it quickly again. This is usually in the form of a paper 'dope' sheet, which shows a diagram of the various controls and switches, which can then be marked by the user for each setting. Supplies of blank sheets are then made available by the makers. A refinement of this system is the cardboard template, which actually fits on top of the control board, with appropriate holes for the controls and switches. This can also be marked and obviously read more quickly. The larger synthesizers have computerized memory functions for instant 'patching'.

A synthesizer can both create sounds and alter them. It can alter either its own or ones that are fed into it via an input (which most models have, though this is something worth checking before buying). There are four principal functions which do this altering:

Filter

This changes the structure of a sound, by filtering its harmonics. In this way the sound of one instrument can be changed into that of another. One of the most effective uses of the filter is to alter its control *while the sound is being passed through it*, so that it is constantly changing from one harmonic extreme to another. This is how the familiar 'wow-wow' sound is made with electric guitars.

Envelope shaper

This shapes a sound, by first chopping it into regular beats, which can be altered in regularity, length of beat and gap, and speed. It can also vary the attack and decay of the pulse which is produced, and alter this from the very gradual fading in or dying away, to a sudden one. This facility is very useful in conjunction with a sound resource unit, since rhythm tapes can be built up, using the complete rhythmic accuracy of the envelope.

Ring modulator

This is in a sense the reverse of a filter, since it mixes two sounds, allowing each to 'treat' the other. The mixing of a voice with another sound is how the BBC 'dalek' voices are produced.

Reverberation

This produces the familiar bathroom echoing effect, and can be adjusted through various degrees. It is by no means found exclusively in the synthesizer, and is often added at the amplifier stage.

Using a synthesizer

The importance of using a synthesizer not as a classroom toy, but as an integral piece of the music department's equipment, has already been stressed. Teachers who attempt to use a synthesizer alone with a full class or even large groups will soon discover the futility of this. There are, however, situations where a synthesizer might be used in apparent isolation.

Either of the main two types of synthesizer may be used with very small groups or individuals who are able and interested enough to get something out of this activity. This is perhaps an ideal situation, but older pupils can often be left alone to experiment, and this can be useful if successful sounds are recorded and put into the sound resource centre. When using the synthesizer with younger classes, there may be opportunities for small groups to do similar work, though this is better organized in conjunction with the main class activity.

A synthesizer clearly has a very useful place in the sound resource unit, since it can produce whichever sounds are required for any particular project. However, it is perhaps better kept as a reference point, and only used when all other sources for a particular sound have been exhausted.

The keyboard type of synthesizer can also be used for almost any performance or activity where a solo instrument can usually be used, since it is able to imitate other instruments as well as create new sounds, all of which can be 'played' with perfect tuning. The more creative aspects of the machine however, mean that it can also be used for experimental classroom music.

Related resources

School textbooks

P. Farmer: *Recording and Electronics* (Longman Music Topics Series) Longman

Other books

T. Dwyer: *Making Electronic Music* (two pupils' books, two records and teacher's handbook) OUP

EAV Ltd.: *Electronic Music* (tape/slide sequence) EAV

R. Orton: *Electronic Music for Schools* CUP

Synthesizer manufacturers

Yamaha Ltd., Kemble/Yamaha Mount Avenue, Bletchley, Milton Keynes MK1 1JE

EMS (Electronic Music Studios), 277 Putney Bridge Road, London SW15 2PT

Roland UK Ltd., Great West Trading Estate, 983 Great West Road, Brentford, Middlesex TW8 9DN

General bibliography

The following books, which are of general interest to music teachers, have been recommended by the contributors in addition to those listed in each of their specialist bibliographies:

Teachers' books and articles

P. Farmer: *Music in the Comprehensive School* OUP, 1979
A personal view of how a truly comprehensive music curriculum should be developed.

G. Russell-Smith: *Be a Real Musician* and *Be a Better Musician* Boosey & Hawkes, 1977
These books contain several activities and games useful for the younger secondary pupil when first developing elementary skills.

E. Szonyi: *Musical Reading and Writing* Boosey & Hawkes, 1974
Three teachers' books and eight pupils' books with progressive activities.

K. Swanwick: *A Basis for Music Education* NFER, 1979
A book which helps to build a philosophy and offers a structure within which to operate.

B. Brocklehurst: 'The Changing Pattern of School Music', *Music Teacher* July, August and September 1980
An assessment of class teaching in the 1970s and suggestions for the future.

G. Reynolds and A. Chatterley: *A Young Teacher's Guide to Class Music* Novello, 1969
A 'back to basics' book not primarily intended for specialists, but still containing much that is useful.

M. Ross (Ed): *The Creative Arts* Heinemann, 1978
A book full of answers to the question, 'Why do we teach creative subjects?'

R. Murray Schafer: *The Composer in the Classroom, Ear Cleaning, The New Soundscape* and *When Worlds Sing* Universal Edition
A series by the Canadian composer containing a wealth of classroom ideas.

W. Whitty and M. Young (Eds): *Explorations in the Politics of School Knowledge* Nafferton Books, 1976
A collection of essays on a wide range of educational subjects, including music, which illustrate the difficulties of creating radical educational change.

Class textbooks

P. Farmer: *Into the Classics, Into the Modern Classics* and *Instruments of the Orchestra* (Longman Music Topics Series) Longman

P. Farmer: *A Handbook of Composers and their Music* OUP

T. Attwood: *Music from Scratch* OUP

J. Bartholomew: *The Steel Band* OUP